AF262961

mushrooms

50 TRIED & TRUE RECIPES

Julia Rutland

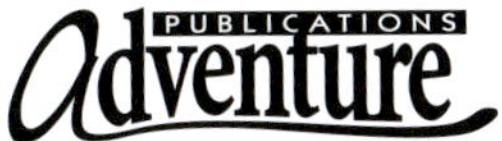

Adventure PUBLICATIONS

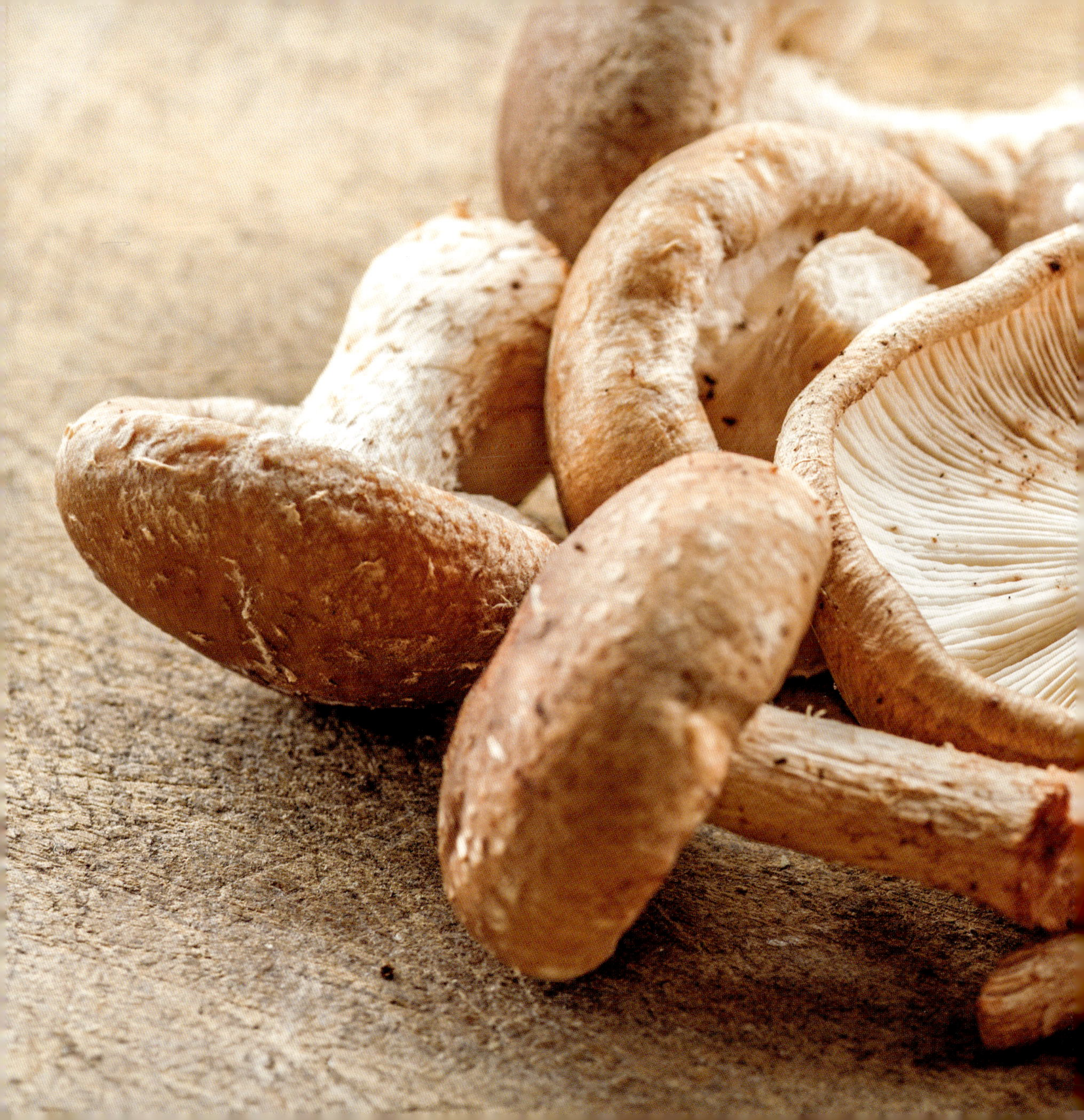

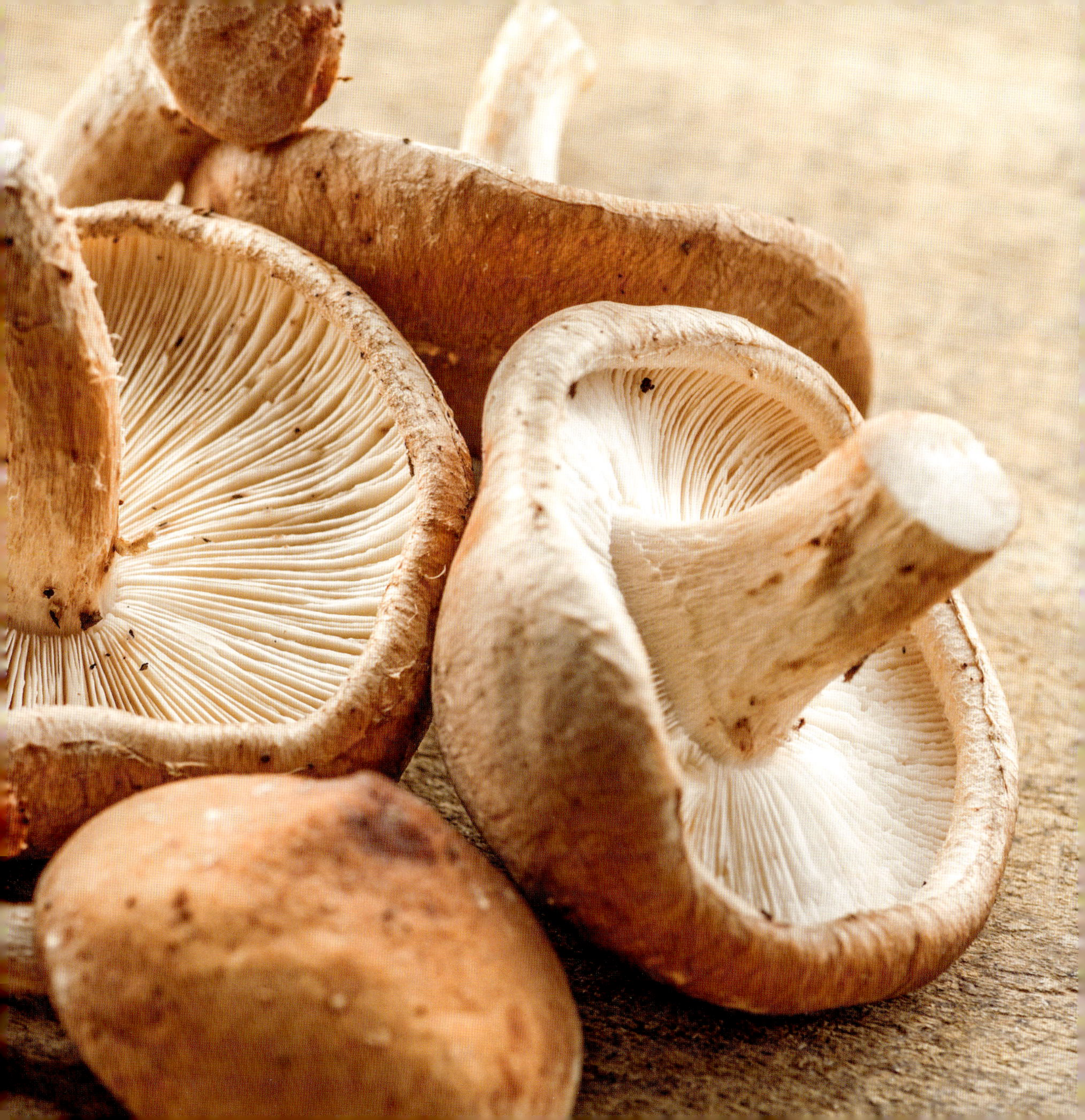

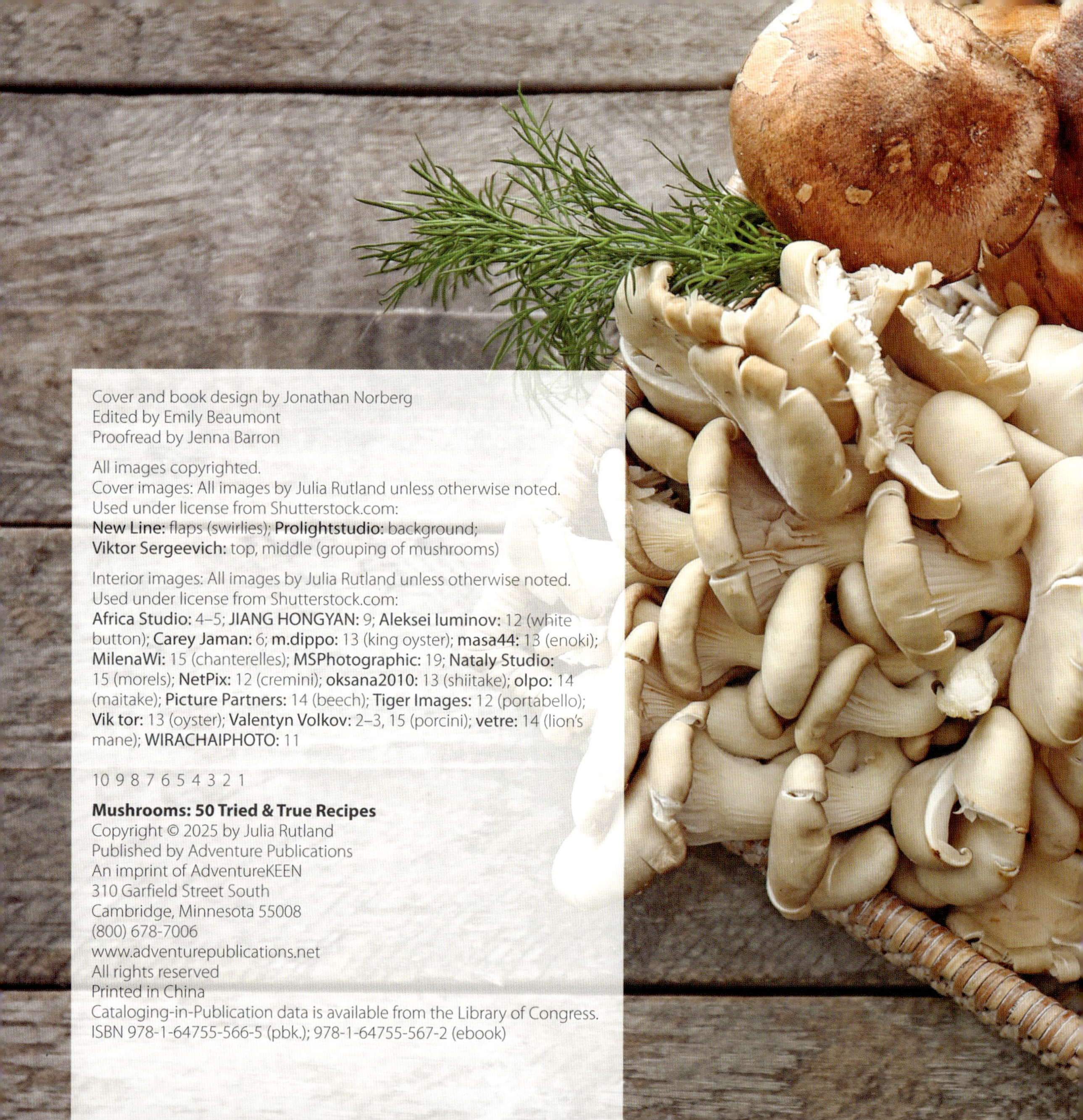

Cover and book design by Jonathan Norberg
Edited by Emily Beaumont
Proofread by Jenna Barron

All images copyrighted.
Cover images: All images by Julia Rutland unless otherwise noted.
Used under license from Shutterstock.com:
New Line: flaps (swirlies); **Prolightstudio:** background;
Viktor Sergeevich: top, middle (grouping of mushrooms)

Interior images: All images by Julia Rutland unless otherwise noted.
Used under license from Shutterstock.com:
Africa Studio: 4–5; JIANG HONGYAN: 9; Aleksei luminov: 12 (white button); Carey Jaman: 6; m.dippo: 13 (king oyster); masa44: 13 (enoki); MilenaWi: 15 (chanterelles); MSPhotographic: 19; Nataly Studio: 15 (morels); NetPix: 12 (cremini); oksana2010: 13 (shiitake); olpo: 14 (maitake); Picture Partners: 14 (beech); Tiger Images: 12 (portabello); Vik tor: 13 (oyster); Valentyn Volkov: 2–3, 15 (porcini); vetre: 14 (lion's mane); WIRACHAIPHOTO: 11

10 9 8 7 6 5 4 3 2 1

Mushrooms: 50 Tried & True Recipes
Copyright © 2025 by Julia Rutland
Published by Adventure Publications
An imprint of AdventureKEEN
310 Garfield Street South
Cambridge, Minnesota 55008
(800) 678-7006
www.adventurepublications.net

All rights reserved

Printed in China
Cataloging-in-Publication data is available from the Library of Congress.
ISBN 978-1-64755-566-5 (pbk.); 978-1-64755-567-2 (ebook)

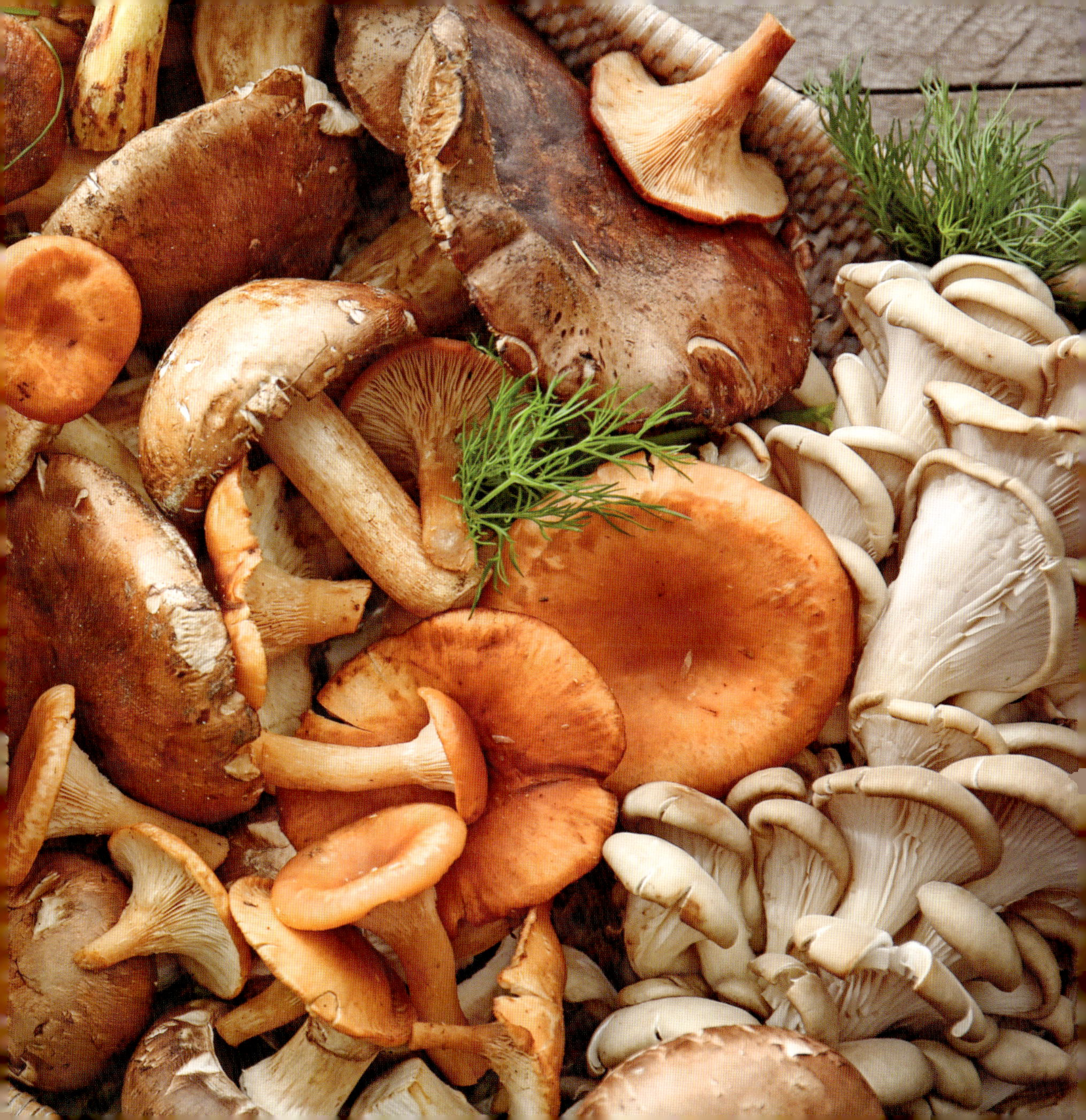

Acknowledgments

To my publishing team, family, and friends—thank you for keeping me grounded like mushrooms on the forest floor. This book wouldn't have sprouted without you!

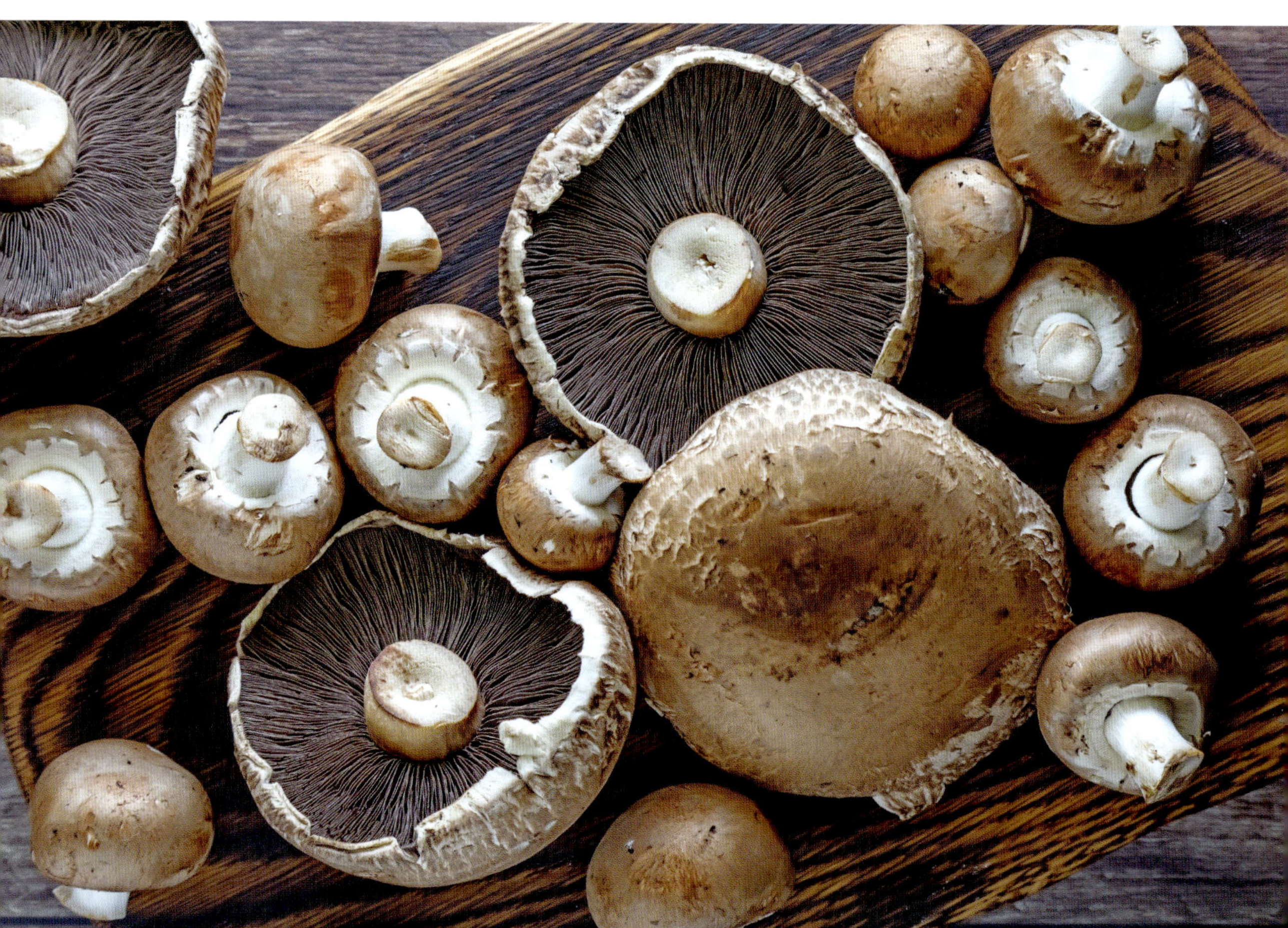

mushrooms

50 TRIED & TRUE RECIPES

Table of Contents

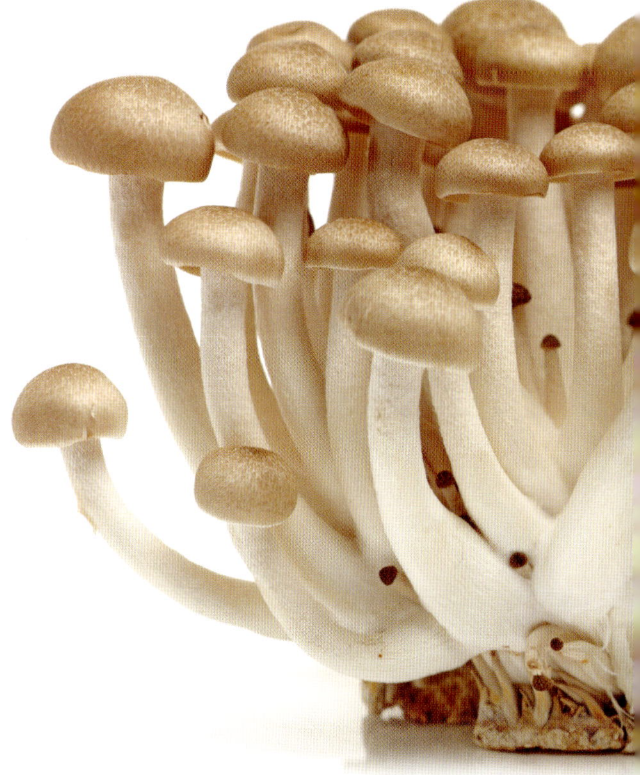

Introduction

This cookbook is a celebration of the many different mushroom varieties available in grocery stores, markets, and international stores. Of course, the old standbys—baby bellas, creminis, and portobellos (all of which are button mushrooms, just at different stages of maturity)—are still the easiest to find, but stores now regularly stock delights such as lion's mane, beech mushrooms, chanterelles, enoki, oysters, and maitake. This book features 50-plus recipes that highlight the incredible range and versatility that store-bought mushrooms have to offer.

About Mushrooms

Mushrooms belong to the kingdom Fungi, a massive group that includes molds, yeasts, mushrooms, and lichen. It might seem strange, but fungi are more closely related to animals than they are to plants, and not all fungi produce mushrooms. There are perhaps 5 million fungi species, but only around 20,000 species produce mushrooms. While a discussion of fungal reproduction would require volumes—it gets complicated—a decidedly simplified summary of mushrooms is possible.

The actual "body" of a mushroom-producing fungus is found below the substrate (what it's growing on). What we know as a "mushroom" is actually a fruiting body: The mushroom produces many spores, which are each capable of producing another fungus (and eventually, more mushrooms). A mushroom is therefore akin to the fruit of a tree, and the fungal mycelium, which often resembles whitish "roots," forms the body of the fungus. The mycelium, in turn, is made of tiny strand-like structures called hyphae. When a mushroom spore lands on a suitable area (often spread by the wind), it starts forming hyphae, which eventually produce mycelia and, if conditions are right, more mushrooms.

Mushrooms play a number of roles in the environment. Some mushrooms are saprobes, decomposers that break down organic matter (such as dead wood or leaf litter). Others are mycelial and have a mutually beneficial relationship with tree and plant roots, enabling nutrient exchange. Others are parasitic upon other organisms, including other mushrooms, at times! These are not hard-and-fast roles, and a mushroom can play multiple roles over the course of its lifetime.

Mushroom Cultivation

Most of the mushrooms that we're familiar with are products of cultivation—mushroom farming, essentially. Most farmed mushrooms are the familiar "button mushrooms" (*Agaricus bisporous*), which are known by several names depending on maturity: cremini, portobello, etc. Other cultivated mushrooms include oysters, shiitake, and lion's mane. Globally, China is far and away the main mushroom producer, followed by the United States, Italy, and Poland. In the United States, Pennsylvania and California produce the most cultivated mushrooms.

Mushroom cultivation is tricky because the grower must essentially replicate the conditions that each mushroom prefers. This is easier for some groups of mushrooms than others. Saprobe mushrooms—those are decomposers—are readily sold in grow-at-home mushroom kits where the mycelium feed on sawdust and begin fruiting when exposed to water. Oyster mushrooms are a famous example. Other mushrooms, including the coveted morel, have proven much harder to cultivate, though there have been recent advances.

Mushroom cultivation can occur indoors or outdoors, depending on the method, but it requires rigorous control of light levels, humidity, airflow, and temperature. Cultivators also must avoid contamination from other fungi.

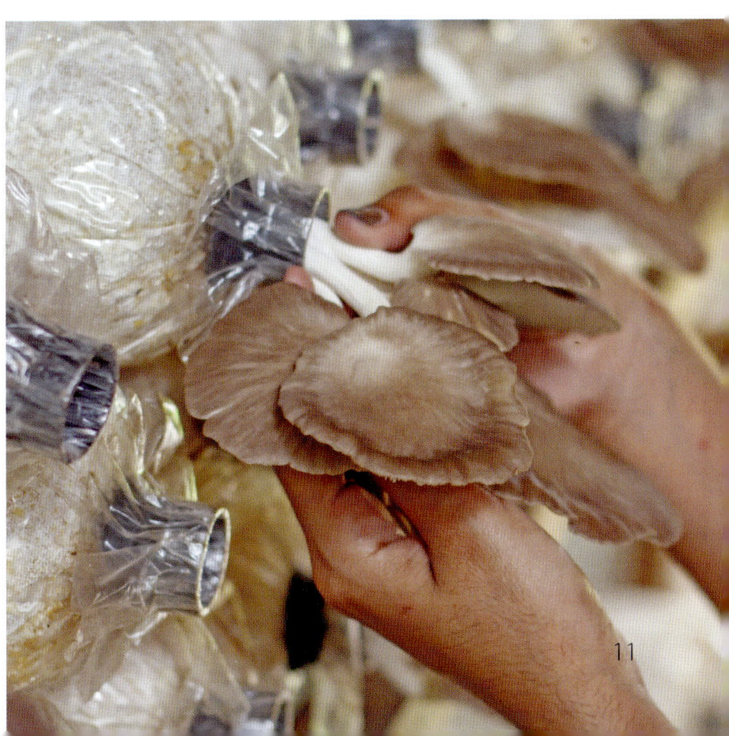

Mushroom Lingo

While some store-bought mushrooms are incredibly common (like button mushrooms), others are more rare. For this book, I'll describe three categories of mushrooms: **cultivated, exotic,** and **wild.**

CULTIVATED

Cultivated mushrooms are grown in a controlled environment, often at a farm or another agriculture-like setting, and conditions are carefully managed. Here are some of the more common cultivated mushrooms:

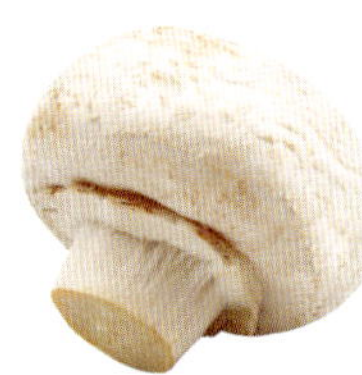

White Button Mushrooms

APPEARANCE: When people think of an edible mushroom, this is usually what they have in mind. Button mushrooms are the same species as cremini and portobello; the difference is how mature they are. White button mushrooms are young. Their caps are smooth, round, and have a thick stem. In cross section, it shows a traditional "mushroom" shape and is common on pizza.

FLAVOR: They're not especially strong and are somewhat meaty in texture.

HOW USED: Incredibly versatile, they can be sautéed in pastas, added to pizzas, used in salads, or added to soups.

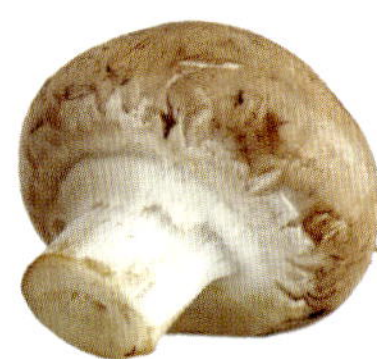

Cremini or Baby Bella Mushrooms

APPEARANCE: Cremini mushrooms are the same species as button mushroom, just more mature. They are larger in size, brown, and with a texture that's a bit more pronounced.

FLAVOR: Cremini have more flavor than button mushrooms and are often described as "earthy."

HOW USED: Cremini mushrooms are great sautéed, roasted, grilled, or fried. They are commonly used in sauces, risottos, soups, and meat dishes like stews.

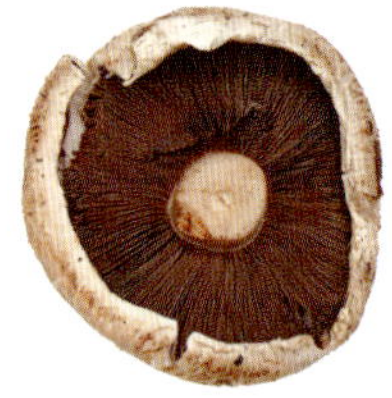

Portobello Mushrooms

APPEARANCE: As the fully mature form of buttons/creminis, these large, flat mushrooms have dark-brown caps with a diameter from 3 to 6 inches.

FLAVOR: They are deep, earthy, and savory with a robust, almost meat-like taste.

HOW USED: Often grilled or roasted, portobello mushrooms are popular as a meat substitute in burgers. They can also be used in pastas and stir-fries or baked and/or stuffed.

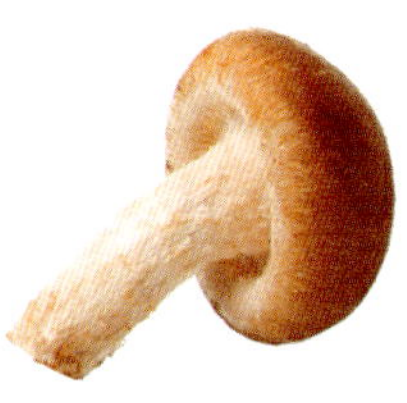

Shiitake Mushrooms

APPEARANCE: Shiitakes have a medium-size cracked cap that is a deep brown with curled or curved edges; the bottom portion of the stem is woody and is often discarded or used in stocks.

FLAVOR: They have a strong, savory flavor with a rich taste.

HOW USED: Native to East Asia, the shiitake is an important part of a number of well-known Asian dishes, including miso soup. Shiitakes are versatile and can be used in soups, pasta, sauces, and stir-fries.

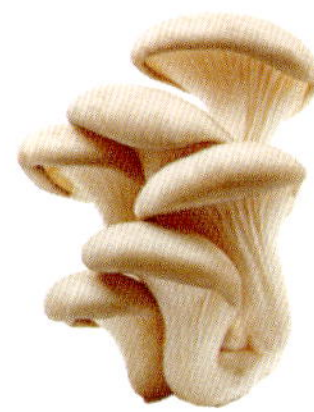

Oyster Mushrooms

APPEARANCE: Oyster mushrooms have overlapping fan-like caps that range from white or cream-colored to gray, yellow, or even pink.

FLAVOR: Oyster mushrooms have a mild, pleasant taste. They get their name because their taste is slightly reminiscent of seafood or oysters. It's definitely subtle and not overpowering. The texture can often be meat-like, making it a good meat substitute.

HOW USED: Oyster mushrooms are great when grilled or roasted, as well as in pastas and stir-fries.

EXOTIC

In this book, "exotic" mushrooms refer to well-known, but not always available, mushroom varieties that offer particular flavors, textures, or appearances. Common exotic mushrooms found in grocery stores include:

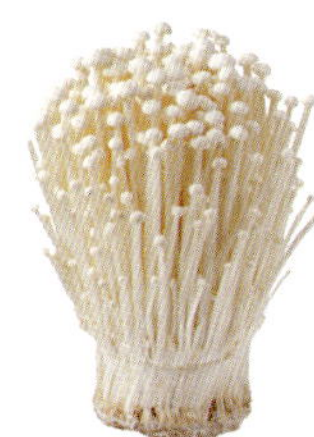

Enoki

APPEARANCE: Enoki mushrooms have long, skinny stems and small caps; they are often sold in bunches or clusters.

FLAVOR: Enokis have a savory, quite mild flavor and a bit of a crunch.

HOW USED: Common in Asian cuisines, enokis are a good option for soups, hot pots, and salads.

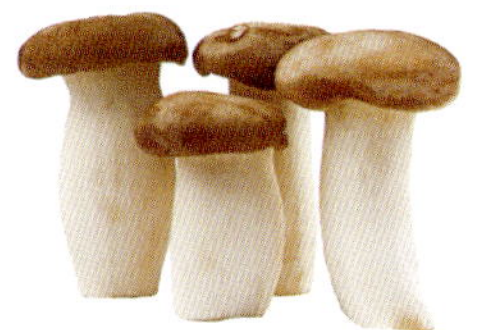

King Oyster or King Trumpet

APPEARANCE: With impressive, thick stems and a relatively small tan cap, this is a spectacular mushroom.

FLAVOR: King oysters have a substantial, meaty texture and an earthy taste that can be scallop-like.

HOW USED: Often used as a meat or shellfish substitute, they can be grilled or sliced; they're also popular in soups, stir-fries, or stews.

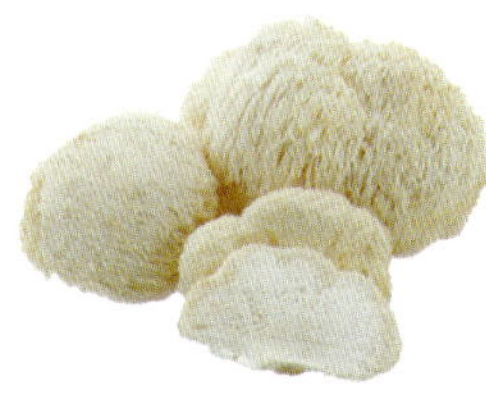

Lion's Mane

APPEARANCE: An unmistakable mushroom, this type has a white, shaggy, stringy or mane-like appearance (hence the common name).

FLAVOR: It's sweet and mild, with a taste often compared to seafood, especially lobster or scallops.

HOW USED: Typically sautéed or grilled, it can be used as "steaks" or in tacos, pastas, or added to many other dishes.

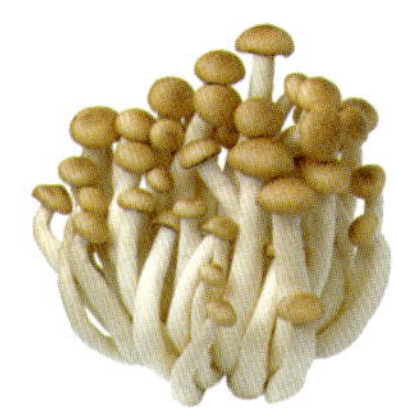

Beech Mushrooms

APPEARANCE: These mushrooms are sold in bunches and have white-to-tan caps and long stems.

FLAVOR: With a somewhat chewy texture and a mild flavor, they can sometimes also add a bit of a crunch.

HOW USED: Beech mushrooms are a good option in pastas, soups, and even salads.

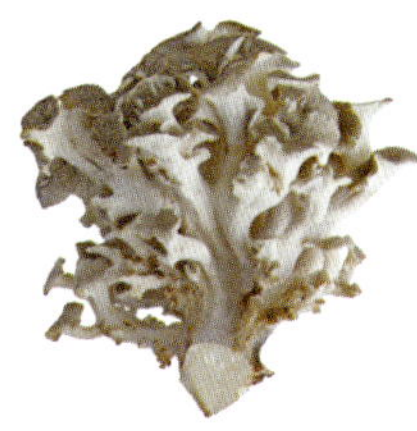

Maitake or Hen-of-the-Woods

APPEARANCE: With large, fan-like clusters that somewhat resemble feathers, this mushroom has an iconic look.

FLAVOR: Hen-of-the-woods is often described as having a nutty or woody flavor and a somewhat meaty texture.

USAGE: Hen-of-the-woods is often roasted or grilled as "steaks," and it works well in tacos and other dishes.

WILD

In this book, "wild mushrooms" refer to foraged mushroom varieties that are sometimes available in grocery stores. These mushrooms are picked by licensed professionals, and the recipes in this book call for such store-bought "wild" mushrooms.

Safety Note: If you substitute your own foraged finds, you must confirm that your identification is correct, be sure that you have ruled out toxic lookalikes, and know that you are preparing the mushrooms in question correctly. Needless to say, this book is not a guide to mushroom identification, and the recipes in this book call explicitly for store-bought mushrooms. Common wild mushrooms include:

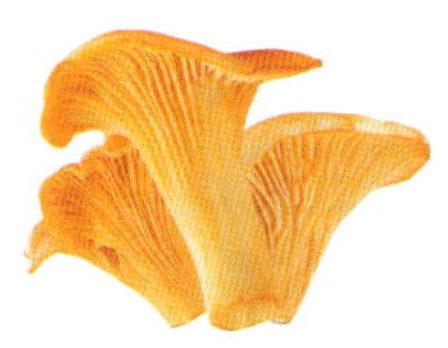

Chanterelles

APPEARANCE: With a striking trumpet shape and a yellow-to-golden color, chantarelles are as beautiful as they are sought-after.

FLAVOR: Chantarelles are often described as having a slightly fruity or nutty flavor.

HOW USED: Used in pastas, soups, stews, or in sauces, they are often sautéed, roasted, or steamed.

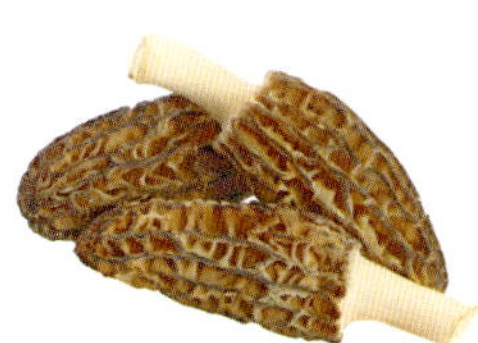

Morels

APPEARANCE: Famous for their pitted caps and sponge-like texture, morel caps range from white to yellow-gold to brown and black. The stems are cream-colored.

FLAVOR: Morels have a pleasant flavor, often described as nutty or earthy.

HOW USED: They are lovely in creamy sauces, soups, risottos, or sautéed with butter.

SAFETY NOTE: Raw morels are toxic, and morels must be thoroughly cooked. Also, when trying a new-to-you mushroom, always try a small portion first (and not mixed with other "new-to-you" mushrooms). That way, if it doesn't sit well with you, you'll be able to identify the culprit.

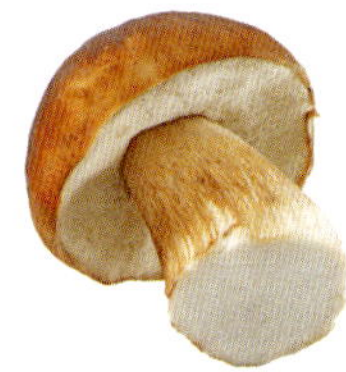

Porcini

APPEARANCE: These thick, impressive mushrooms have pronounced, bulbous stems and thick tan-to-brownish-red caps. Porcini have pores instead of gills on the underside of their caps.

FLAVOR: Porcini have an impressive flavor that is often described as woodsy and rich.

HOW USED: Porcini make a wonderful soup or stew base and work well as a main component of creamy sauces. They're also a good option for pastas or risottos.

Nutrition and Health Benefits

Mushrooms are a low-calorie, nutrient-rich food, and they contain some compounds not typically found in other grocery store fare. According to the USDA, a typical serving of button mushrooms has just 31 calories but 2.9 grams of protein, 2 grams of fiber, and very little fat; they are a good source of potassium, magnesium, zinc, and selenium. These numbers are typical of other mushroom varieties as well.

Per the Mayo Clinic, mushrooms are also a great source of vitamin D, which is important for bone and tooth health, and they're also linked to lower levels of dementia and Type 2 diabetes. Regular consumption of mushrooms may also significantly lower cancer risk, and some mushrooms—especially lion's mane—have been studied for neuroprotective effects and brain health.

Purchasing Mushrooms

Before buying a package of mushrooms, inspect them carefully. They shouldn't be discolored or have an "off" smell. A fresh, earthy smell is what you're after.

- Look for mushrooms that are firm and round. Avoid those that are mushy or have caps or stems that appear dried out or brittle. (Unless you're buying dried mushrooms, of course; those need to be reconstituted, however.)

- Avoid discoloration. Store-bought mushrooms should generally have a uniform coloration, so avoid those with blemishes or serious discoloration. Also, if a mushroom is slimy or damp, avoid it, and be on the lookout for condensation inside mushroom packages, as it's a sign that those mushrooms may spoil quickly.

- Should caps be open or closed? Mushrooms with a closed cap are younger and will have a milder flavor; those with an open cap will generally have a more intense flavor.

- Do they need to be uniform in size? For stuffed mushrooms or pickup appetizers, smaller mushrooms are easier to prepare and serve. Choose mushrooms that are similar in size for more consistent cooking. If using uneven sizes, quarter or slice for even cooking.

- Buy in small quantities. Mushrooms are best when used fresh, so it's a good idea to buy only what you'll need within a few days.

Storage

- Storing mushrooms properly helps maintain their freshness, flavor, and texture. The best way to store mushrooms is in a paper bag, which allows the mushrooms to "breathe." The vegetable or crisper drawer is ideal, as it has good airflow and a controlled humidity level.

- If you don't have a paper bag handy, you can store mushrooms in a shallow container lined with a paper towel. Place the mushrooms in a single layer and cover them loosely with another paper towel to absorb excess moisture.

- Fresh whole mushrooms, stored properly, can last for around 5 to 7 days in the refrigerator. Presliced mushrooms stay fresh for 3 to 5 days. Cooked mushrooms can be stored in an airtight container in the refrigerator for 3 days.

- Avoid storing mushrooms in plastic, as this traps moisture and can cause them to become slimy and spoil quickly. If possible, store mushrooms whole rather than sliced, as whole mushrooms last longer. Presliced mushrooms have a shorter shelf life due to more exposure to air.

- Raw mushrooms don't freeze well because they contain a lot of water and will become mushy when thawed. If you want to freeze mushrooms, slice and cook them until liquid evaporates. Cool completely and then store in an airtight container up to 9 months. Use cooked frozen mushrooms in soups, stir-fries, and as a pizza topping.

Cleaning

Washing mushrooms properly is key to maintaining their texture and flavor. Here's the best way:

- Use a damp paper towel or soft brush. For mushrooms that are mostly clean, like button, cremini, or portobello, gently wipe them with a damp paper towel.

- Rinse quickly under cold water. If visible dirt (most likely the compost they were grown in) appears, rinse mushrooms quickly under cold water and drain in a colander. Do not soak mushrooms—they easily absorb water and can become soggy and mushy as well as take longer to cook.

- Dry mushrooms immediately. After rinsing, spread mushrooms out on a clean kitchen towel or paper towels; let air-dry or pat them dry gently.

- Trim stems, if necessary. Older button and particular types, such as shiitakes and portobellos, tend to have tough or dry stems. Remove tough or discolored portions with a knife.

- Consider removing the gills from portobello or very large cremini mushrooms. The gills, dark feathery ribbons underneath the cap, can release a dark liquid during cooking that can make the dish appear unappetizing. The gills may have a slightly bitter flavor, and they can trap debris. Scrape the dark gills away with a small spoon and discard, if desired.

Cooking Tips

- Cut or slice mushrooms into even pieces so they cook uniformly. If your package of mushrooms has a wide variety of sizes, quarter large or extra-large mushrooms so the pieces are about the same size as the smallest whole mushroom.

- Avoid overcrowding a skillet or pan, so mushrooms brown and release moisture instead of steam.

- Grilling enhances a mushroom's natural umami flavor and works best with large ones like portobellos. Save skinny or small mushrooms for roasting or sautéing because they are likely to fall through the grill grates.

- Each type of mushroom—button, shiitake, cremini, and portobello—has a unique texture and flavor that can be enhanced by different cooking methods. Button mushrooms have a mild flavor and high water content, so sautéing helps them release their moisture and concentrate their flavor. Roasting enhances their natural sweetness and brings out a slightly crispy texture.

- Cremini mushrooms have a slightly deeper flavor than button mushrooms, and sautéing helps them develop a rich, earthy taste. Grilling gives them a smoky flavor and meaty texture.

- Eat them raw or cooked? Thoroughly cook shiitake, porcini, and especially morel mushrooms (which are toxic uncooked) because eating them raw can cause digestive upset or an allergic reaction. Beech mushrooms tend to taste bitter when raw, so eat those cooked. White or button and enoki mushrooms are mild to delicate and are commonly served raw in salads; however, many health benefits are derived when mushrooms are cooked. In addition, digestibility and flavor are enhanced by cooking.

- Dried mushrooms, such as porcini, are rehydrated and used in soups, risottos, and sauces to add a concentrated umami flavor.

- Lion's mane should be parboiled before using in dishes like crab cakes or pasta dishes. Shred the mushroom with your hands and simmer in a small amount of liquid until tender. Searing or sautéing enhances its texture and brings out its natural sweetness.

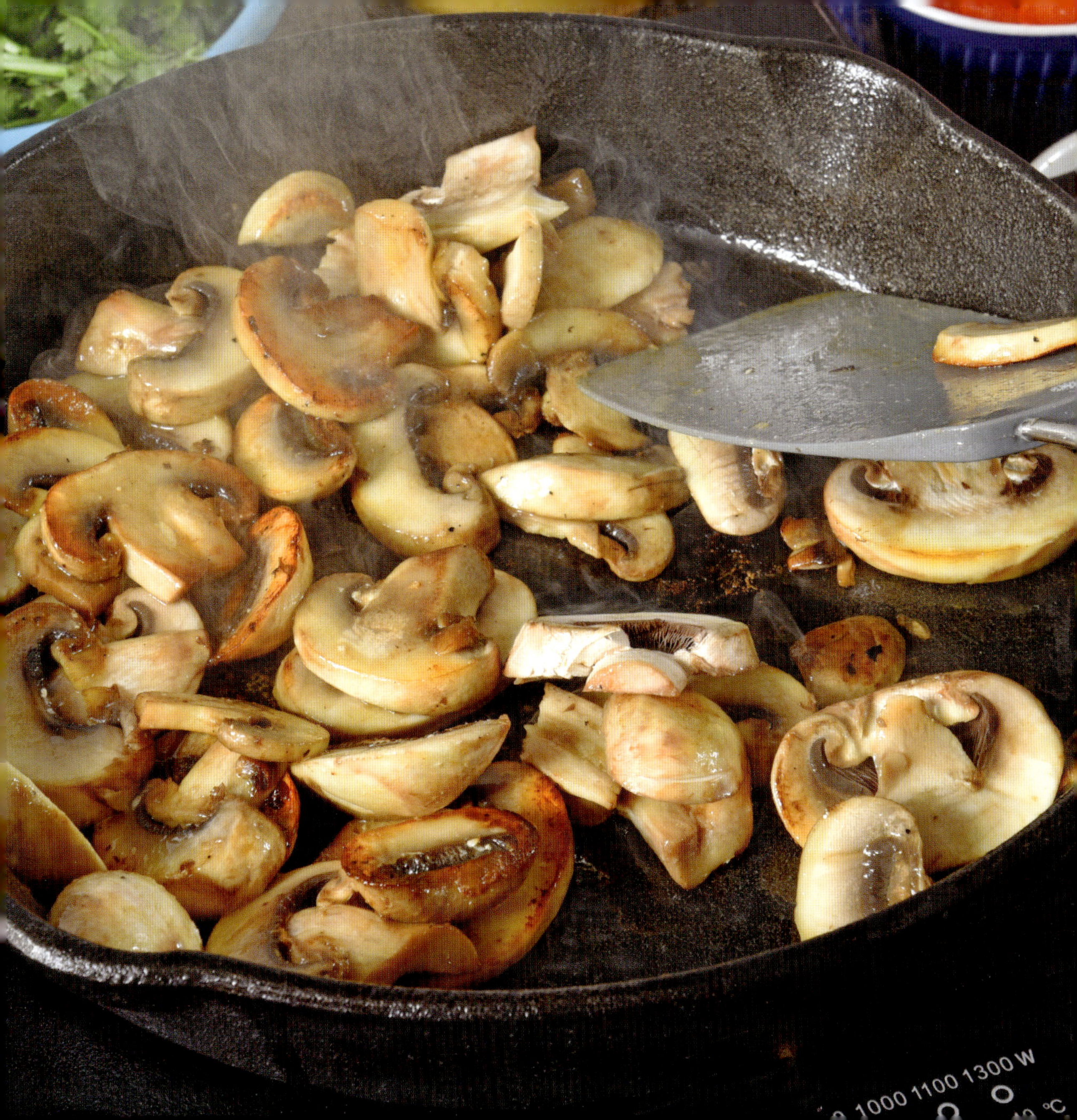

1000 1100 1300 W
°C

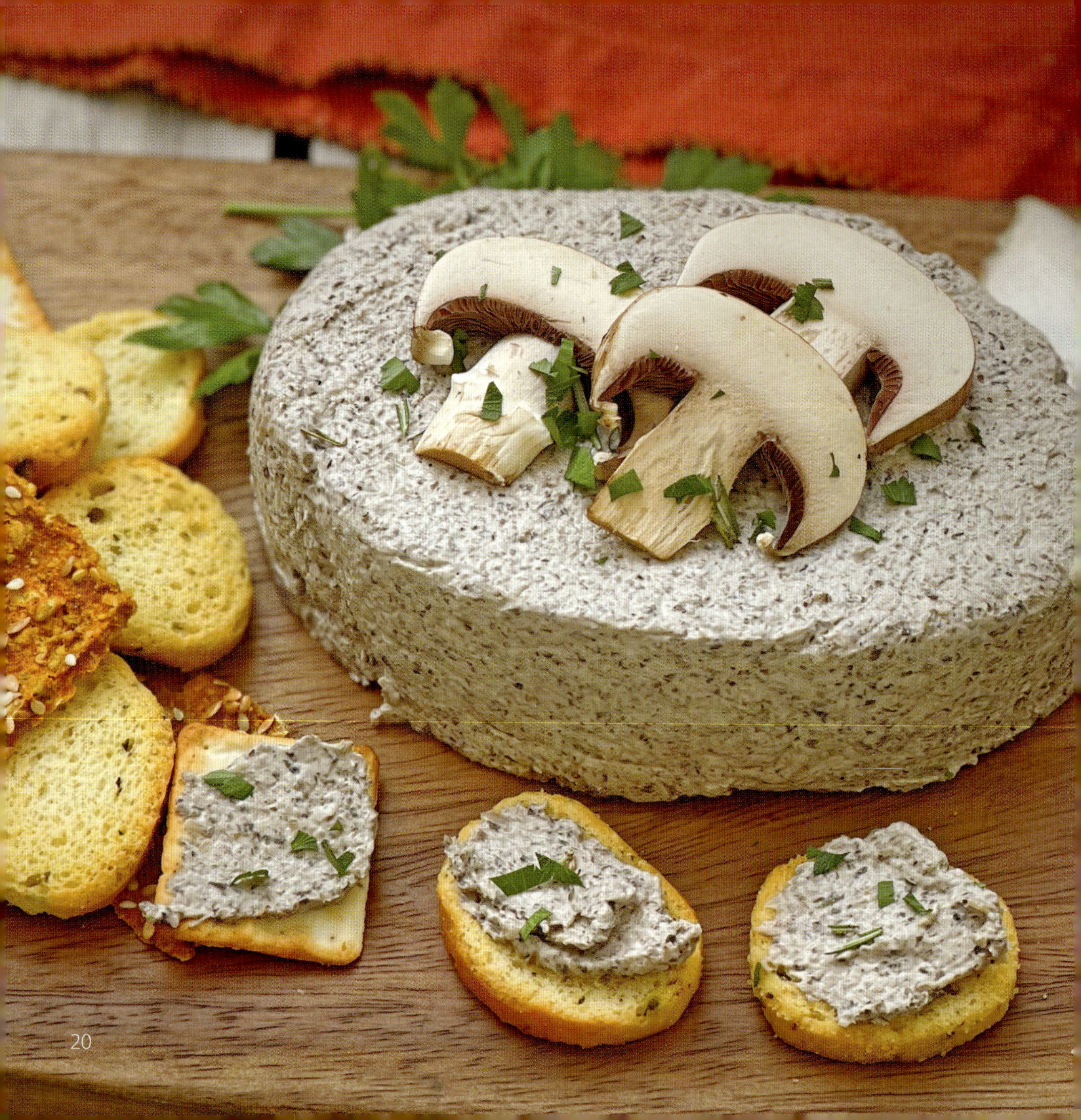

appetizers

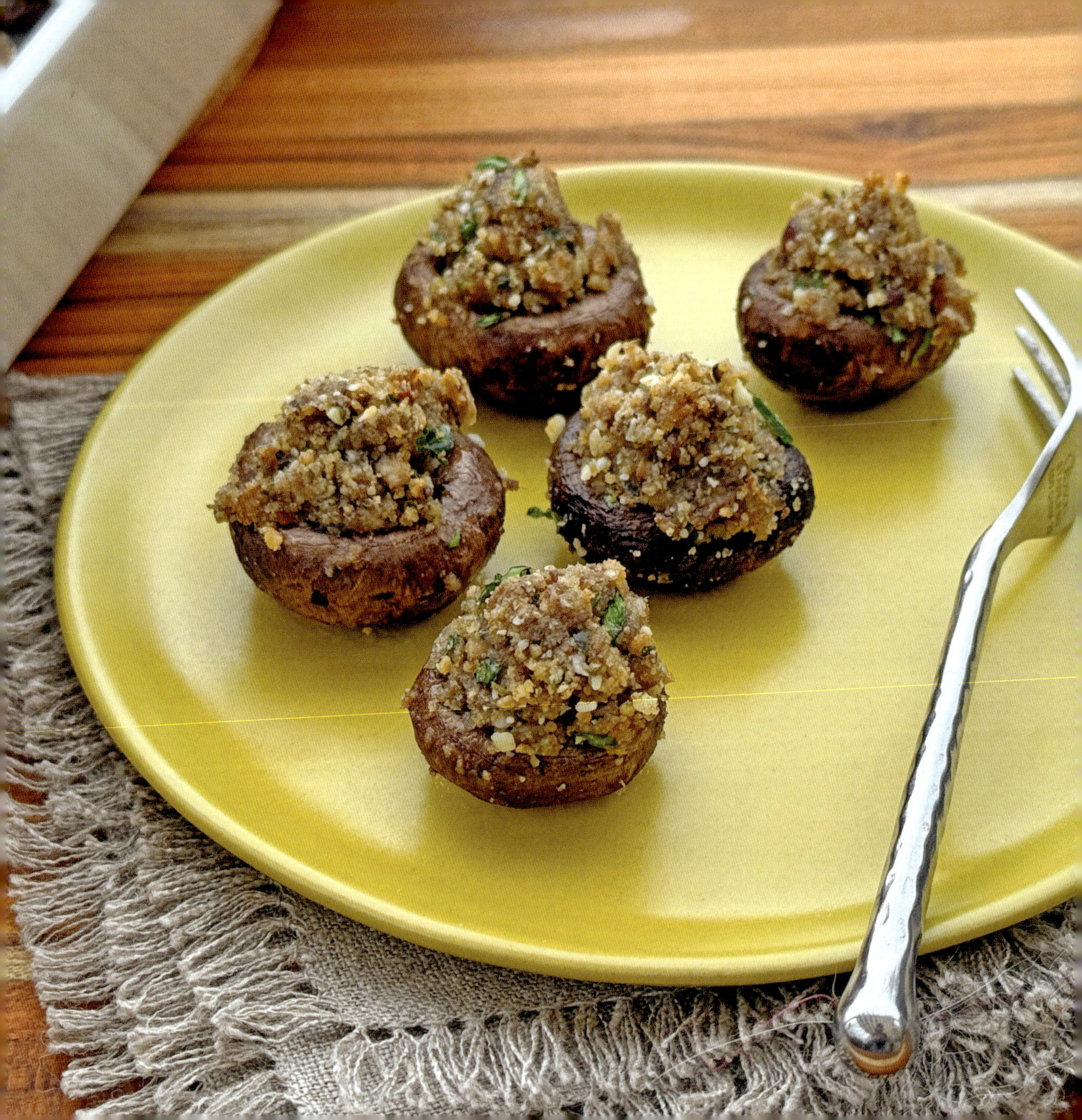

Stuffed Mushrooms

These basic stuffed mushrooms make a timeless appetizer that's simple to prepare yet packed with flavor. Tender mushroom caps are filled with a savory mixture of chopped mushroom stems, buttery breadcrumbs, and earthy cheeses, then baked to perfection. Appropriate for casual gatherings or elegant dinner parties, these bite-size delights can be made ahead and baked just before serving.

makes 1½ dozen

INGREDIENTS

1 pound small button or
   cremini mushrooms
2 tablespoons unsalted or
   salted butter
1 shallot, minced
¼ teaspoon fine sea salt
¼ teaspoon coarsely ground
   black pepper
1 tablespoon soft goat cheese or
   cream cheese
¼ cup seasoned or
   plain fine breadcrumbs
¼ cup (1 ounce) freshly grated
   Parmesan cheese
2 teaspoons chopped
   fresh parsley

Preheat oven to 375°.

Trim any dirty edges of mushroom stems and discard. Remove stems and finely chop (to yield about 1 cup). Brush caps clean and place, cup side down, on a rimmed baking sheet. Bake for 10 minutes or until caps start to soften and liquid exudes. Set aside.

Melt butter in a skillet over medium heat. Add chopped stems, shallot, salt, and pepper. Cook, stirring frequently, until mushrooms are tender and dry. Stir in goat cheese, breadcrumbs, Parmesan cheese, and parsley.

Mound filling evenly inside caps. Return to oven and bake for 10 to 15 minutes or until tender and browned.

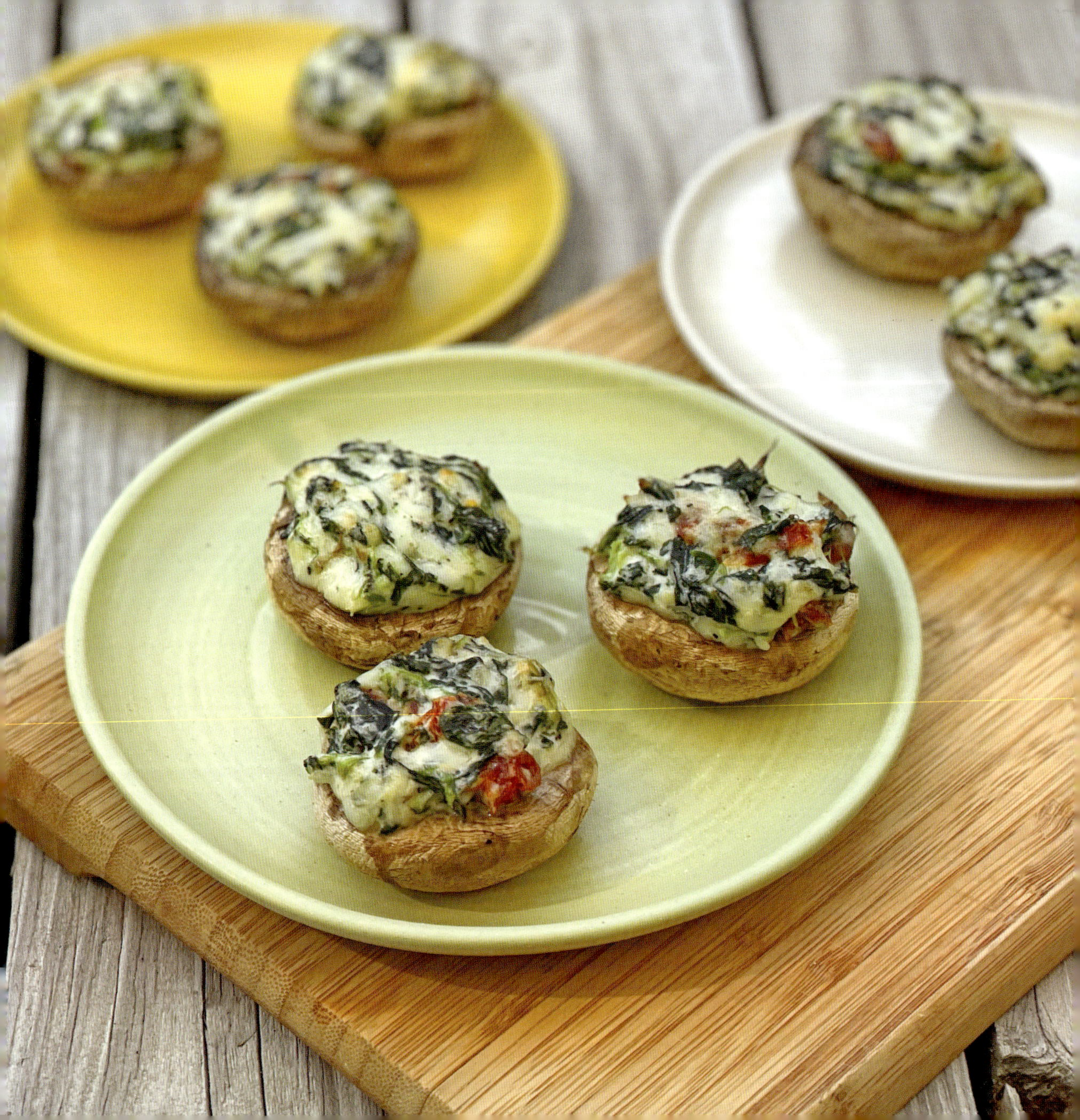

Spinach-, Tomato-, and Cheese-Stuffed Mushrooms

This filling little snack is gluten-free, keto-friendly, and vegetarian, making it a
great choice for get-togethers when you don't know if any guests are on special diets.
You can easily measure a cup of frozen spinach when you buy it chopped and loose in the bag,
rather than the type that is frozen into a block. Measure before it thaws because it will shrink significantly.
Some stores sell mushroom caps ready for stuffing—with stems removed and uniform in size.
If buying a carton of miscellaneously sized mushrooms, you may get more or less than a dozen.

makes 1 dozen

INGREDIENTS

12 large mushrooms
 (about 1 pound)
1 cup frozen spinach, thawed
 and well drained
½ (8-ounce) package cream
 cheese, softened
¼ cup slivered sun-dried
 tomatoes in oil, drained
1 cup (4 ounces) shredded
 mozzarella cheese
¼ teaspoon fine sea salt
¼ teaspoon coarsely ground
 black pepper

Preheat oven to 400°. Remove stems from caps; save for another use or discard. Place, cap side up, on a rimmed baking sheet lined with parchment paper or aluminum foil. Bake for 10 minutes.

Meanwhile, combine spinach, cream cheese, tomatoes, mozzarella, salt, and pepper in a medium-size bowl, stirring until well blended.

Turn mushroom caps over, draining any liquid that collects. Mound filling evenly inside caps.

Return to oven and bake for 17 to 20 minutes or until golden brown and tender.

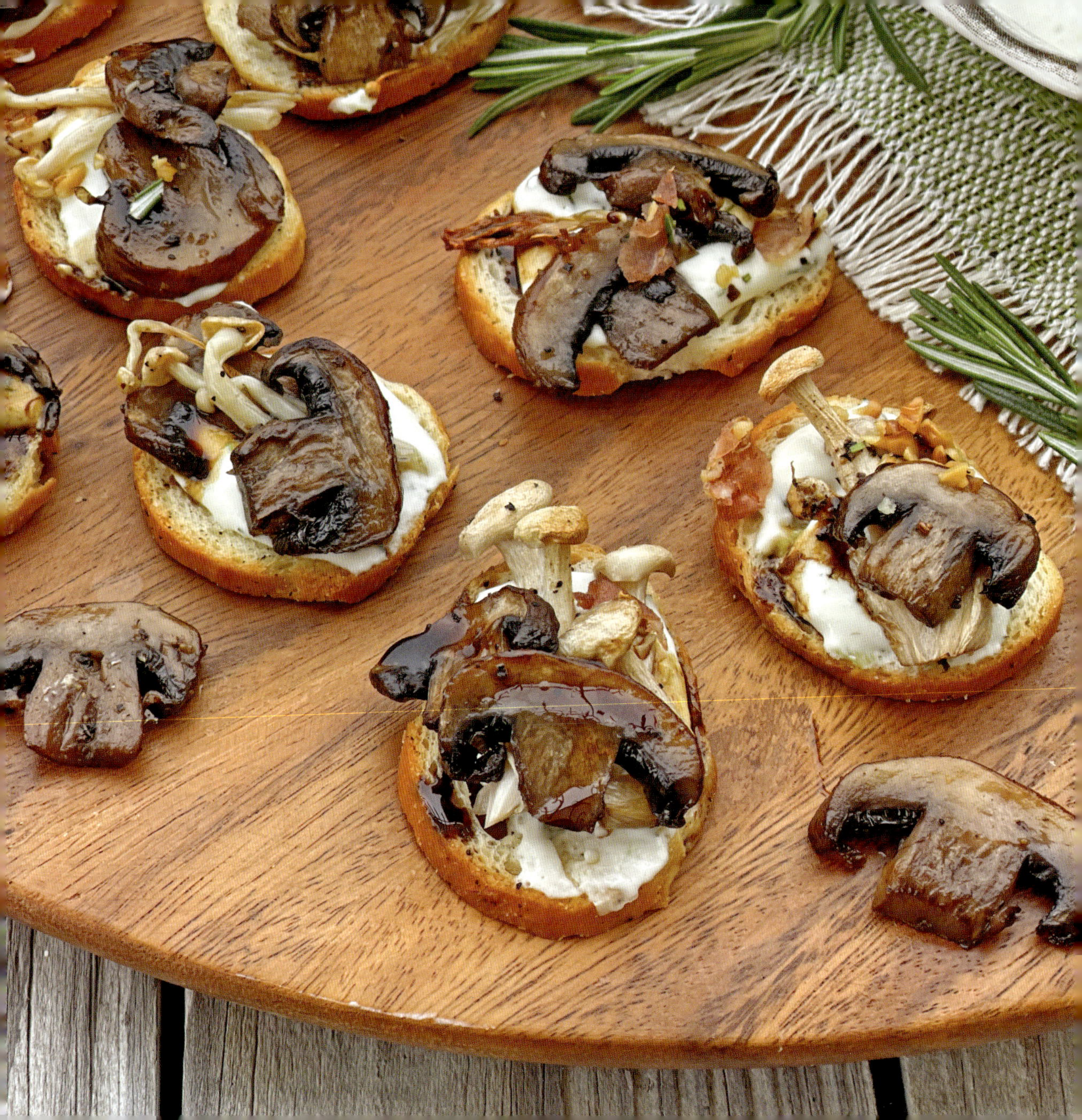

Roasted Mushroom Crostini with Herbed Ricotta and Balsamic Glaze

Assemble immediately before serving, or let guests compile their own, as the ricotta could make the crostini soggy if made ahead.

makes 12 servings

INGREDIENTS

1 pound mixed mushrooms (cremini, shiitake), sliced

Olive oil

1 teaspoon fine sea salt, divided

½ teaspoon coarsely ground black pepper

⅓ cup toasted and finely chopped walnuts

1½ ounces thinly sliced prosciutto, chopped

1 teaspoon finely chopped fresh rosemary

1 cup whole milk ricotta cheese, drained if necessary

1 tablespoon chopped fresh dill, parsley, or basil

1 teaspoon lemon juice

2 green onions, finely chopped

½ garlic clove, minced

Toasted Baguette Slices (recipe at right)

Balsamic Glaze (recipe at right)

Preheat oven to 400°. Place mushrooms on a rimmed baking sheet. Drizzle with olive oil and sprinkle with ¾ teaspoon salt and pepper, stirring to coat; spread out in a single layer. Bake for 30 to 40 minutes, stirring occasionally, until mushrooms are golden and caramelized.

Meanwhile, combine walnuts, prosciutto, and rosemary in a small bowl; set aside. Combine ricotta, dill, lemon juice, green onions, and garlic in a bowl. Stir in remaining ¼ teaspoon salt.

Spread whipped ricotta mixture onto each Toasted Baguette Slice. Top with roasted mushrooms and walnut mixture. Drizzle with Balsamic Glaze.

Toasted Baguette Slices: Slice **1 (12- to 16-ounce) French baguette** ¼-inch thick. Brush both sides with **olive oil.** Spread in a single layer on a baking sheet and bake at 400° for 4 minutes. Turn slices over and bake for 4 minutes or until golden brown.

Balsamic Glaze: Combine **½ cup balsamic vinegar** and **2 teaspoons light brown sugar** in a saucepan. Bring to a boil, reduce heat, and simmer over medium-low heat until reduced by half. Cool. Makes ¼ cup.

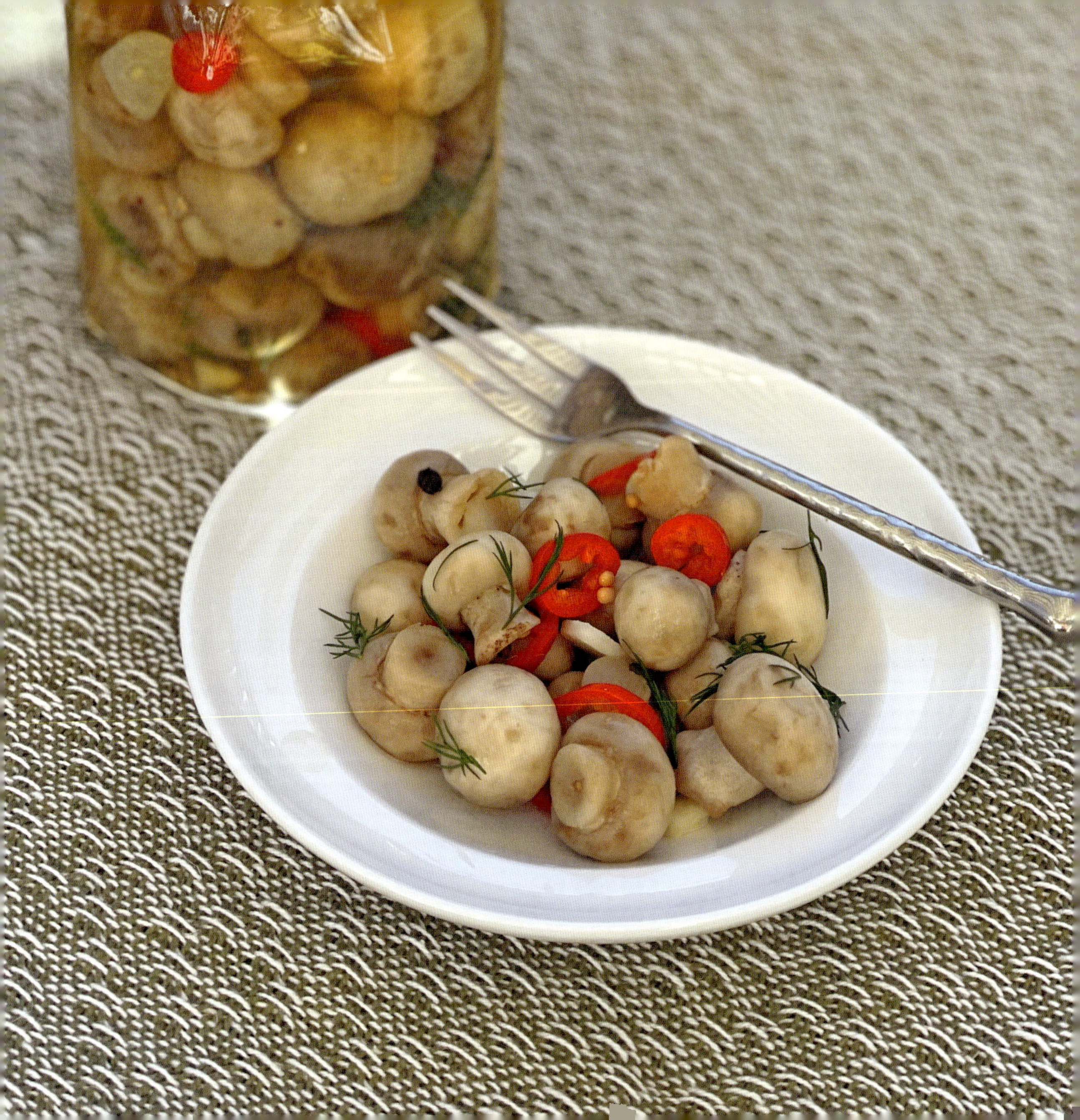

Pickled Button Mushrooms

Serve alongside cheeses and meats on a charcuterie tray, or stir into pasta salads.
This treat is best when the mushrooms are allowed to absorb the flavors for at least a day in the refrigerator.
Chill for up to a month, keeping mushrooms completely submerged in brine.

makes about 4 cups

INGREDIENTS

1 pound petite or very small button mushrooms, cleaned and trimmed
1 cup water
½ cup white vinegar
3 garlic cloves, thinly sliced
1 red jalapeño or other chili pepper, thinly sliced
1 tablespoon kosher salt
2 teaspoons whole black peppercorns
2 teaspoons mustard seeds
2 teaspoons granulated sugar
2 bay leaves
2 sprigs fresh dill, leaves torn from stems

Cook mushrooms in boiling water for 5 minutes; drain and set aside.

Combine 1 cup water, vinegar, garlic, red jalapeño, kosher salt, peppercorns, mustard seeds, sugar, and bay leaves in a large saucepan. Bring to a simmer over medium heat, stirring until sugar and salt are fully dissolved.

Add blanched mushrooms to vinegar mixture, stirring until well blended. Simmer for 5 to 7 minutes. Remove from heat and stir in dill.

Transfer mushrooms and brine to several small (or one large) sterilized jars. Make sure brine completely covers mushrooms. Let cool to room temperature, then cover and refrigerate. Discard bay leaves before serving.

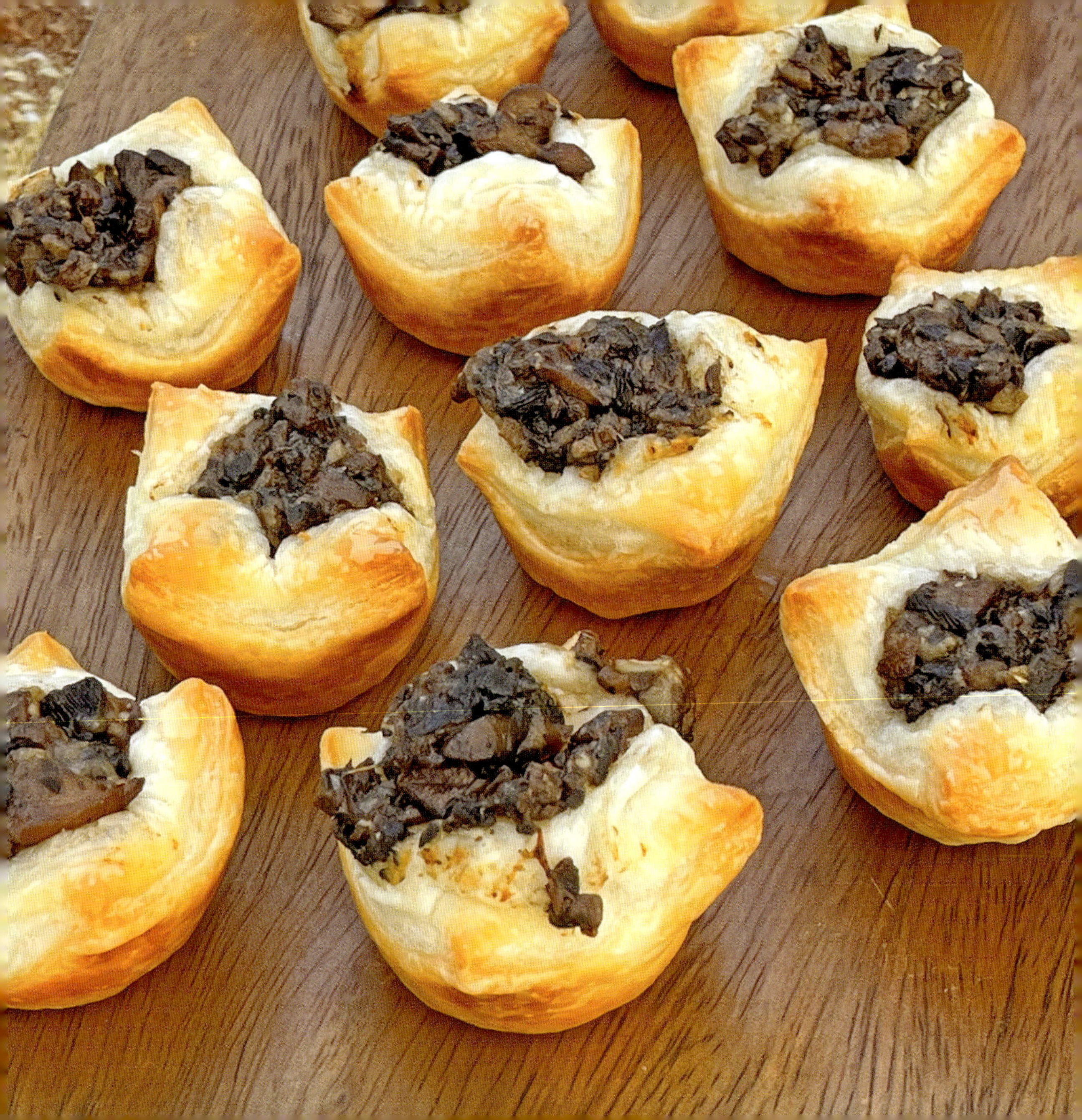

Mushroom Puffs

This delightful bite-size appetizer is made with flaky puff pastry and a savory mushroom filling. Quick and easy to prepare in a mini-muffin pan, they're perfect for parties or as an elegant snack.

makes about 18 puffs

INGREDIENTS

1 tablespoon salted or
    unsalted butter
8 ounces cremini, shiitake,
    or button mushrooms,
    finely chopped
2 garlic cloves, minced
⅛ teaspoon dried thyme
¼ cup heavy whipping cream
¼ cup (1 ounce) freshly grated
    Parmesan cheese
¼ teaspoon fine sea salt
¼ teaspoon coarsely ground
    black pepper
1 sheet refrigerated or frozen-
    and-thawed puff pastry
All-purpose flour

Preheat oven to 400°. Lightly grease a mini-muffin pan with butter.

Melt 1 tablespoon butter in a skillet over medium heat. Add mushrooms, garlic, and thyme. Cook, stirring frequently, for 8 to 10 minutes or until mushrooms are tender and liquid evaporates.

Stir in cream and cook, stirring constantly, for 2 minutes or until thickened. Stir in Parmesan cheese, salt, and pepper. Set aside to cool slightly.

Roll puff pastry sheet out onto a lightly floured surface to remove creases. Cut pastry into 2½-inch squares. Gently press squares into cups of prepared pan, allowing edges to overhang. Spoon about 1 heaping teaspoon mushroom mixture into each cup.

Bake for 15 minutes or until pastry is golden and puffed. Remove from oven and let stand until cool enough to remove from pan.

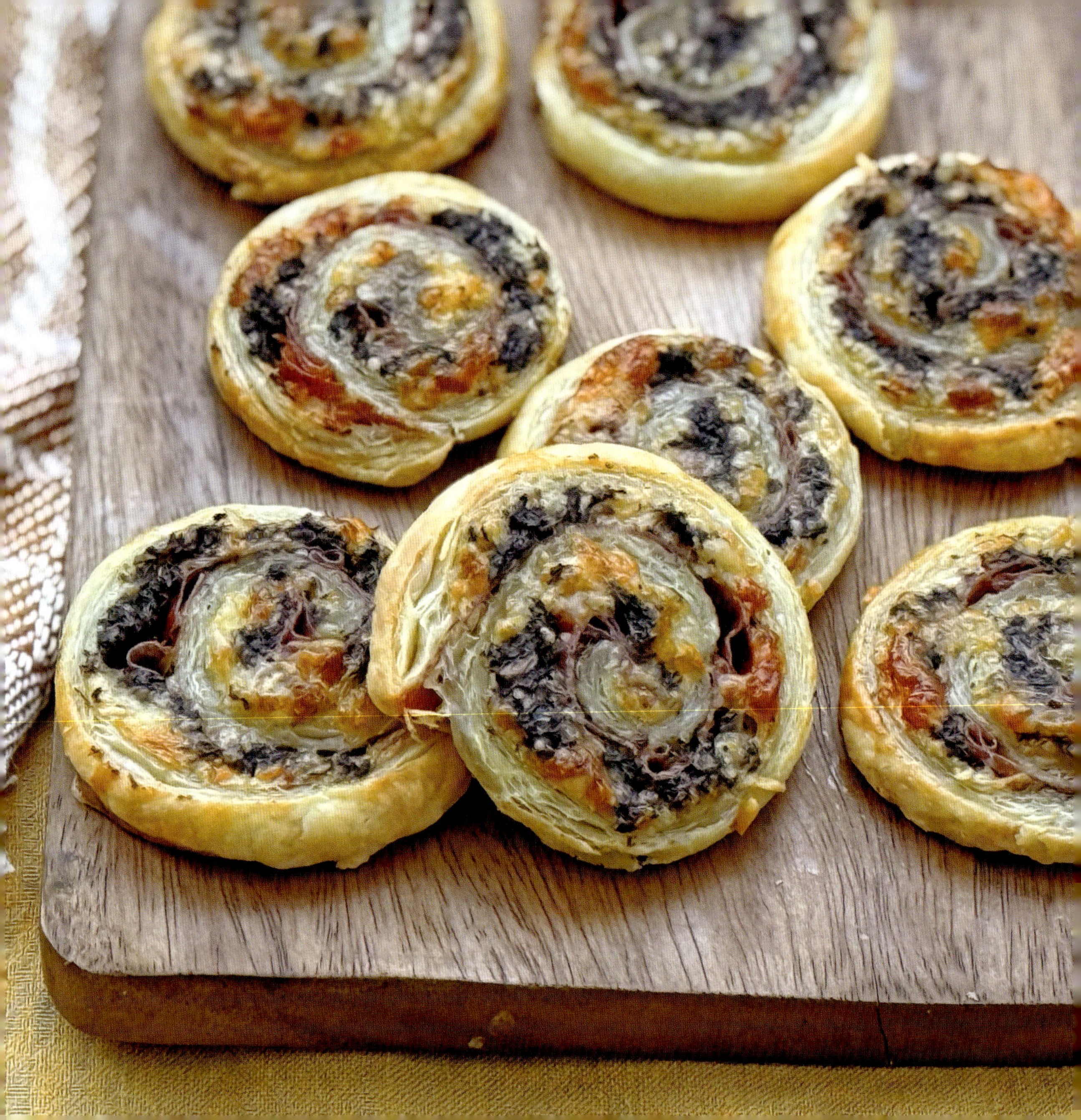

Mushroom Puff Pastry Pinwheels

These savory pinwheels are the perfect bite-size treat for any occasion, from casual gatherings to elegant soirées. Easy to prepare and irresistibly delicious, they can be made ahead and baked fresh for a warm appetizer guests will love.

makes about 1½ dozen

INGREDIENTS

1 teaspoon olive oil
8 ounces cremini, button, or other mushrooms, finely chopped
2 garlic cloves, minced
½ teaspoon dried thyme
⅛ teaspoon fine sea salt
⅛ teaspoon coarsely ground black pepper
1 sheet refrigerated or frozen-and-thawed puff pastry
All-purpose flour
½ cup (2 ounces) freshly grated Parmesan cheese
½ cup (2 ounces) shredded mozzarella cheese
8 to 10 slices salami or prosciutto, thinly sliced
1 egg, beaten
1 tablespoon water

Preheat oven to 400°. Line a baking sheet with parchment paper or nonstick aluminum foil.

Heat olive oil in a skillet over medium heat. Add mushrooms, garlic, thyme, salt, and pepper. Cook, stirring frequently, for 8 to 10 minutes or until mushrooms release moisture and begin to brown. Remove from heat and let cool slightly.

Roll out puff pastry sheet on a lightly floured surface to smooth any creases. Spread mushroom mixture evenly over pastry, leaving a ½-inch border around edges.

Sprinkle Parmesan and mozzarella evenly over mushrooms. Lay slices of salami or prosciutto over cheese.

Roll puff pastry into a tight log, seam side down. Slice log into ½-inch-thick pinwheels and arrange on prepared baking sheet, leaving about 1 inch of space between each piece.

Whisk together egg and 1 tablespoon water. Brush tops of pinwheels with egg mixture. Bake for 15 minutes or until puff pastry is golden and crisp. Let pinwheels cool slightly before serving.

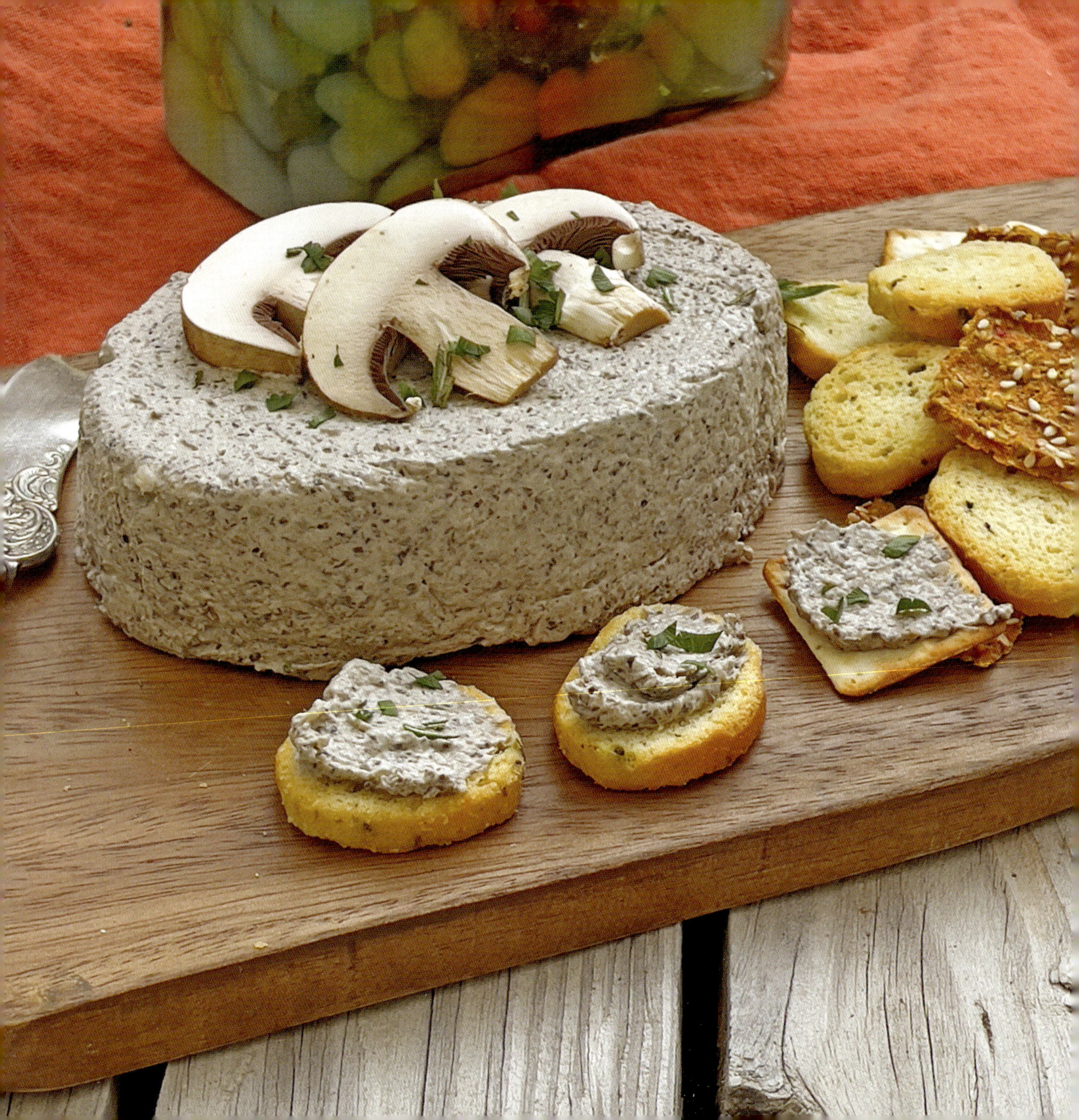

Mushroom Pâté

This rich-and-savory vegetarian pâté is a perfect addition to any party spread.
It's incredibly easy to make yet delivers sophisticated flavors with a blend of earthy
mushrooms and a hint of garlic and rosemary. The recipe yields a generous amount,
ideal for serving a crowd, and can be made ahead of time, allowing the flavors to meld beautifully.

makes 2 cups (12 to 16 servings)

INGREDIENTS

2 (8-ounce) packages button or
  cremini mushrooms, sliced
3 tablespoons salted or
  unsalted butter
3 garlic cloves, minced
2 teaspoons chopped
  fresh rosemary
¾ teaspoon fine sea salt
½ teaspoon coarsely ground
  black pepper
1 (8-ounce) package cream
  cheese, softened
Toasted French bread slices
  or crackers

GARNISHES

reserved mushroom slices,
  fresh parsley leaves

Set aside 2 or 3 mushroom slices for garnish, if desired. Melt butter in a large skillet over medium heat. Add mushrooms, garlic, rosemary, salt, and pepper. Cook, stirring frequently, for 5 minutes or until mushrooms are tender and any liquid exuded evaporates.

Combine mushroom mixture and cream cheese in a food processor. Process until very smooth.

Line a 2- to 3-cup terrine, mini-loaf pan, or bowl with plastic wrap. Spoon mushroom mixture into prepared container, smoothing top. Cover and refrigerate for 2 or more hours or until firm.

Unmold pâté onto a serving plate. Serve with toasted bread slices or crackers. Garnish, if desired.

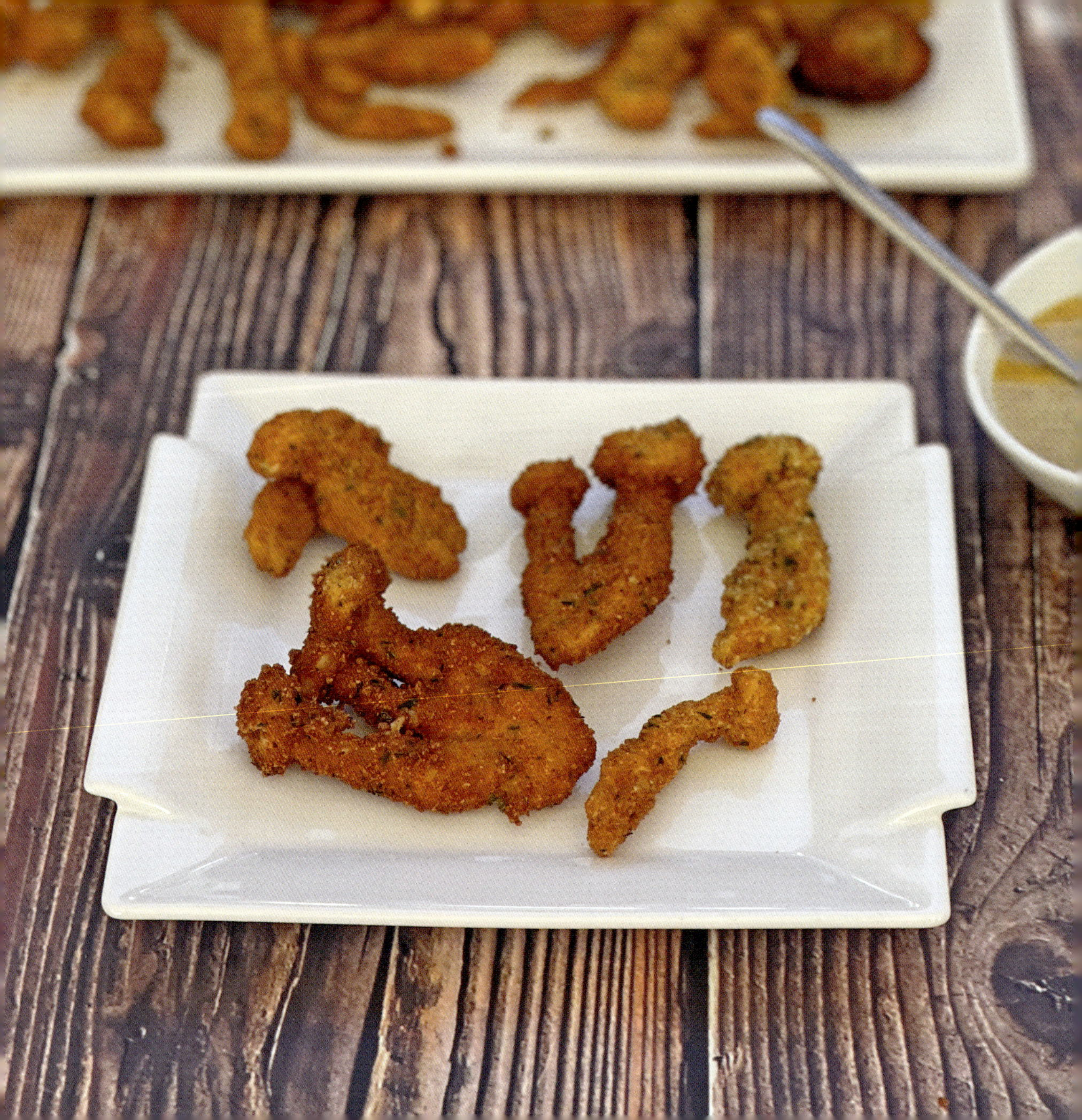

Fried Beech Mushrooms with Honey-Mustard Sauce

Beech mushrooms, with their delicate caps and mildly sweet flavor, are perfect for frying, but you can substitute button mushrooms.

makes 4 servings

INGREDIENTS

1 pound beech or other mushrooms, broken apart or cut into bite-size pieces
½ cup cake or all-purpose flour
1 teaspoon paprika
1 teaspoon garlic powder
¼ teaspoon onion powder
1 teaspoon Italian seasoning
½ teaspoon fine sea salt
2 large eggs
2 tablespoons water
1 cup seasoned fine breadcrumbs
Vegetable oil
Honey-Mustard Sauce (recipe at right)

Clean mushrooms with a damp cloth and trim stems, if necessary. You can leave smaller mushrooms whole or cut larger mushrooms in half or quarters.

Combine flour, paprika, garlic powder, onion powder, Italian seasoning, and salt in a small bowl. Whisk together eggs and 2 tablespoons water in another small bowl. Place breadcrumbs in another small bowl.

Dredge each mushroom in flour mixture, dip in egg mixture, and roll in breadcrumbs, pressing lightly so crumbs adhere.

Pour about 2 inches vegetable oil into a saucepan or deep skillet. Heat oil over medium heat until it reaches 350°.

Fry in batches (don't crowd in pan) for about 2 to 3 minutes or until golden brown and crispy. (If using button mushrooms, fry for about 4 minutes or until done). Serve immediately with Honey-Mustard Sauce.

Honey-Mustard Sauce: Whisk together **¼ cup Dijon mustard, 3 tablespoons honey, 3 tablespoons mayonnaise, 1 teaspoon lemon juice,** and a **pinch of salt** in a small bowl. Makes ½ cup.

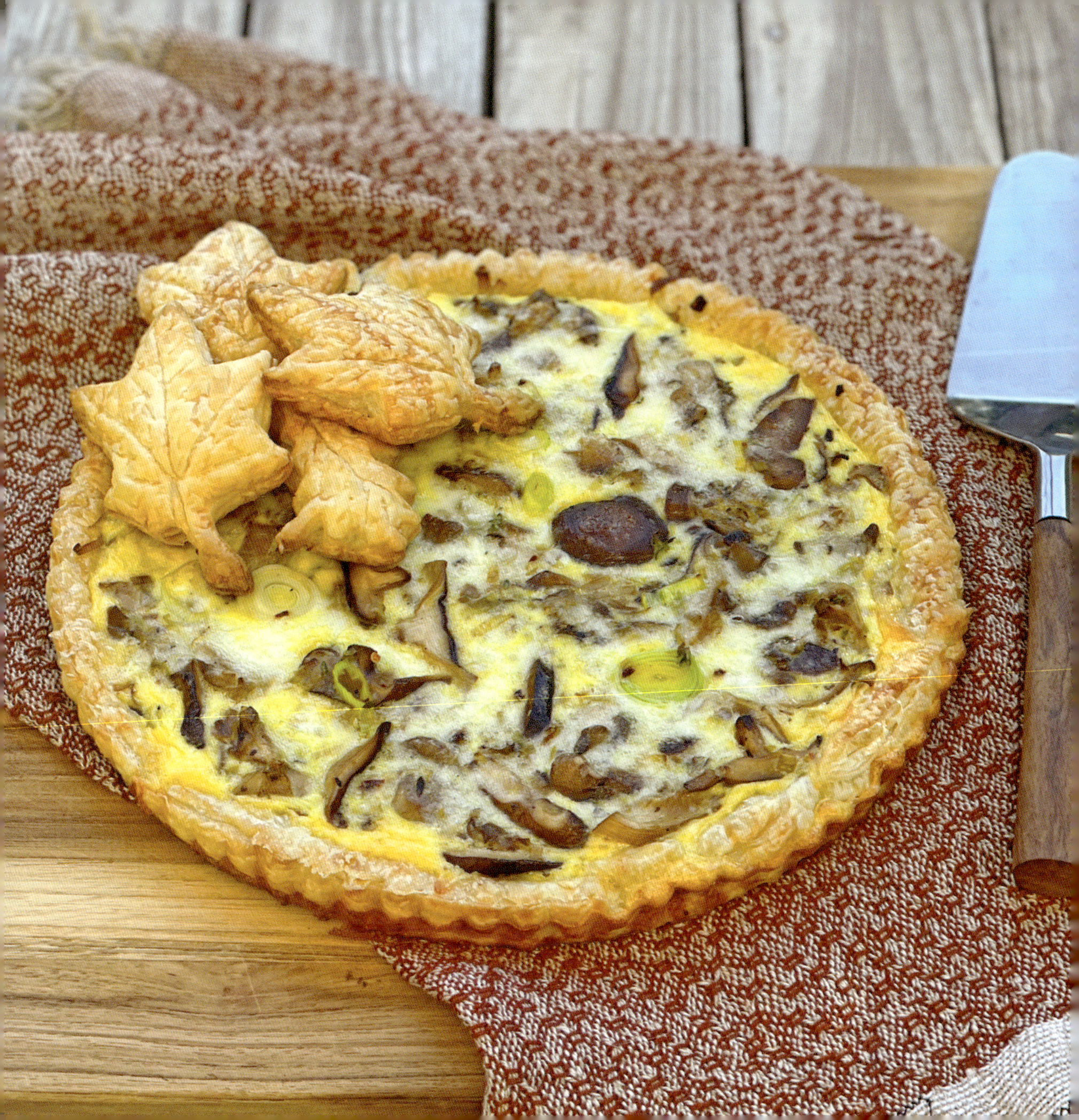

Leek-and-Chanterelle Tart

The pastry is blind baked to ensure a crisp, golden base that complements the savory topping.

makes 6 servings

INGREDIENTS

1 refrigerated or frozen-and-
   thawed puff pastry sheet

All-purpose flour

1 tablespoon extra-virgin olive oil

1 tablespoon unsalted or
   salted butter

⅛ teaspoon crushed red
   pepper flakes

1 large leek, white and light-
   green parts only, thinly sliced

10 to 12 ounces chanterelle or
   shiitake mushrooms, sliced

2 garlic cloves, minced

2 tablespoons fresh thyme leaves

½ teaspoon fine sea salt

¼ teaspoon coarsely ground
   black pepper

2 large eggs

½ cup heavy whipping cream

½ cup (2 ounces) shredded
   Fontina or Gruyère cheese

Preheat oven to 375°. Cut an 11-inch circle out of parchment paper and line an 11-inch tart pan.

Roll out pastry onto a lightly floured surface to fit the inside of the tart pan, trimming and patching edges, if necessary. Prick pastry with a fork. Bake for 10 minutes or until golden brown. Remove from oven and set aside.

Heat olive oil and butter in a skillet over medium heat. Add pepper flakes and leek. Cook, stirring frequently, for 5 to 7 minutes or until softened. Add mushrooms and cook for 7 minutes or until starting to brown and liquid evaporates. Stir in garlic, thyme, salt, and pepper; cook for 1 minute. Set aside.

Whisk together eggs, cream, and cheese in a bowl.

Spread mushroom mixture over baked pastry. Pour egg mixture over mushroom mixture, spreading evenly.

Bake for 20 to 25 minutes or until center is set and top is golden brown.

Note: If sides of pastry slide down when baked, egg mixture might seep under crust. If using a metal tart pan with a remov-able bottom, wrap outside of tart pan with aluminum foil.

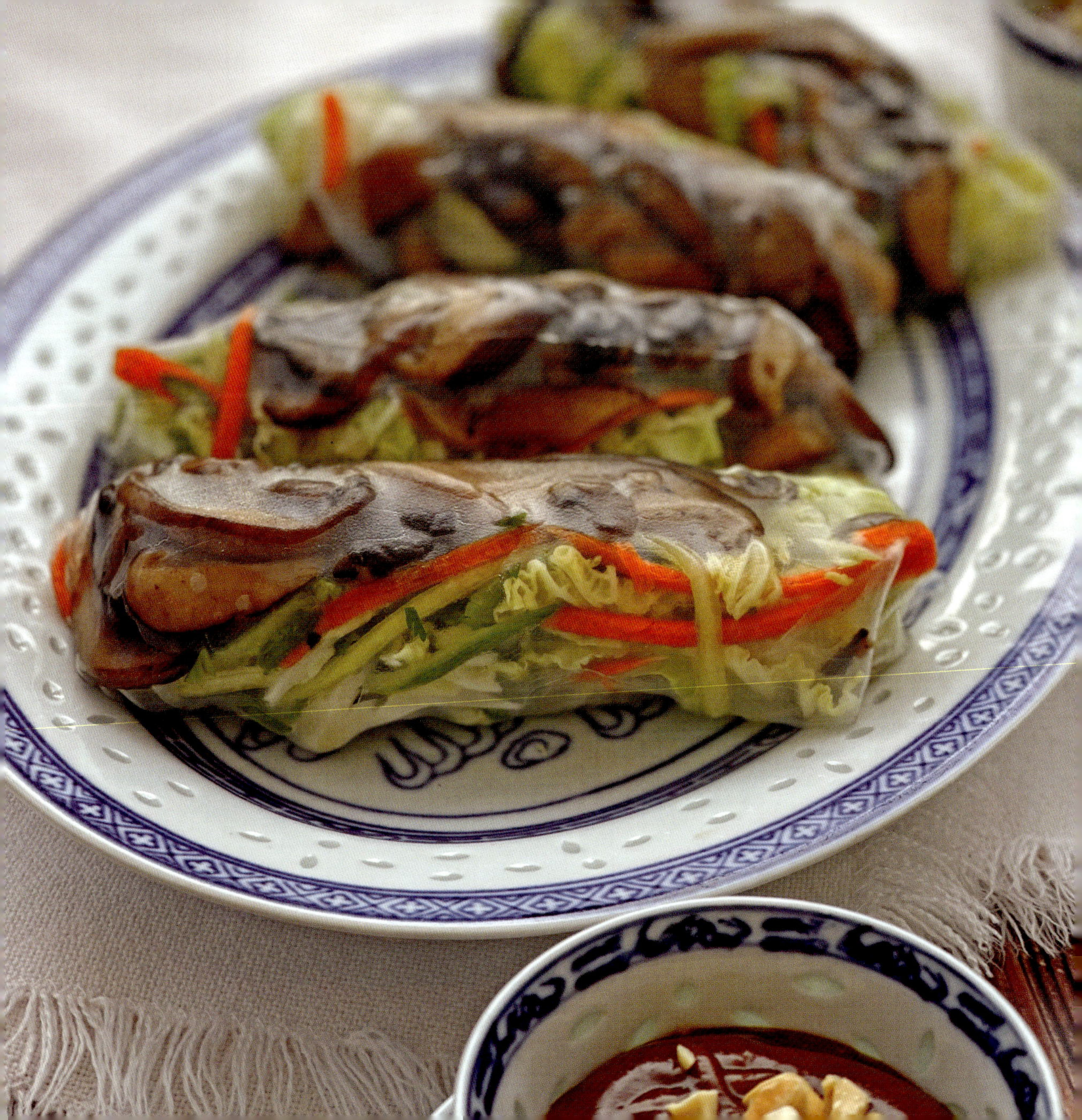

Oyster-and-Shiitake Summer Rolls

These light, refreshing summer rolls bring together the earthy savoriness of sautéed oyster and shiitake mushrooms with the crisp, vibrant crunch of fresh vegetables. Wrapped in delicate rice paper, the rolls are paired with a creamy dipping sauce that balances sweet, salty, and umami flavors.

makes 8 rolls

INGREDIENTS

1 tablespoon sesame oil
12 to 16 ounces oyster and
   shiitake mushrooms, sliced
1 garlic clove, minced
1 tablespoon soy sauce
1 teaspoon rice vinegar
¼ teaspoon coarsely ground
   black pepper
4 cups shredded savoy cabbage
1 small carrot, julienned
   or grated
1 small cucumber, seeded and
   julienned or grated
¼ cup fresh cilantro leaves
8 rice paper wrappers
Hoisin-Peanut Dipping Sauce
   (recipe at right)

Heat oil in a skillet over medium heat. Add mushrooms and garlic. Cook, stirring constantly, for 4 to 5 minutes or until softened. Stir in 1 tablespoon soy sauce, 1 teaspoon rice vinegar, and pepper. Set aside to cool.

Combine cabbage, carrot, cucumber, and cilantro in a large bowl.

Fill a shallow dish with warm water. Dip one rice paper wrapper into water and let soften for about 10 to 15 seconds or until pliable.

Place wrapper on a flat surface and top with about 1 cup cabbage mixture. Top with one-eighth mushroom mixture. Fold sides of wrapper inward, then tightly roll wrapper from bottom, enclosing filling. Repeat with remaining wrappers, cabbage mixture, and mushroom mixture.

Arrange on a platter and serve with Hoisin-Peanut Dipping Sauce.

Hoisin-Peanut Dipping Sauce: Combine **⅓ cup hoisin sauce, 2 tablespoons peanut butter, 1 tablespoon soy sauce, 1 tablespoon rice vinegar,** and **1 tablespoon water** in a small bowl. Makes ½ cup.

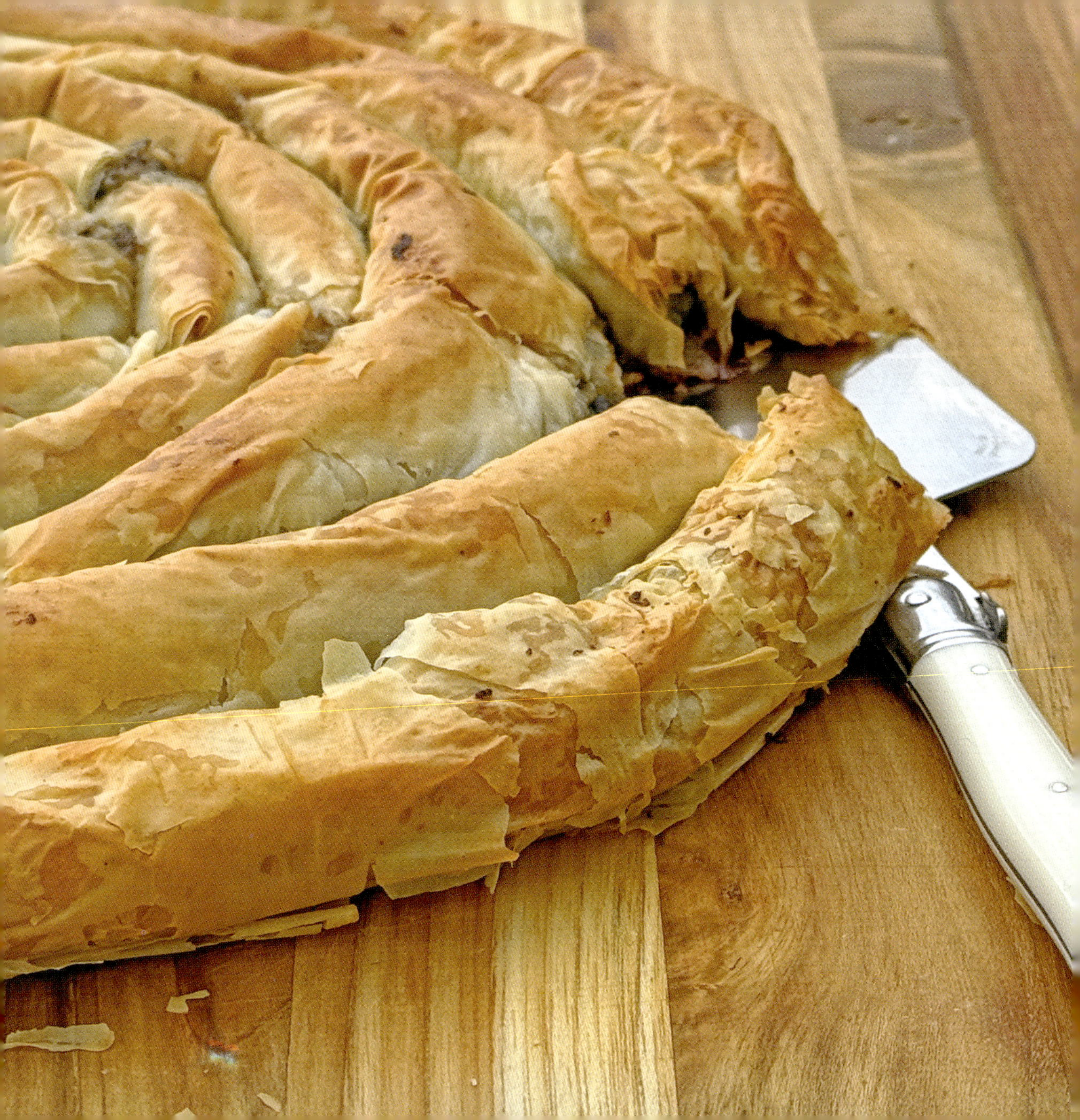

Mushroom-Feta Spanakopita Spiral

Don't let the spiral shape intimidate you— although it might seem tedious,
it's surprisingly simple to assemble and guaranteed to impress!

makes 6 servings

INGREDIENTS

1 tablespoon extra-virgin
  olive oil
1 pound fresh button or assorted
  mushrooms, finely chopped
4 green onions, finely diced
½ teaspoon fine sea salt
½ teaspoon coarsely ground
  black pepper
9 ounces fresh spinach, chopped
1½ tablespoons fresh dill,
  chopped
7 ounces feta cheese, crumbled
¼ teaspoon nutmeg
¾ (16-ounce) package phyllo
  dough, thawed
½ cup (1 stick) salted or
  unsalted butter, melted

Preheat oven to 375°. Line a baking sheet with parchment paper or nonstick aluminum foil.

Heat oil in a large skillet over medium heat. Add mushrooms, green onions, salt, and pepper. Cook, stirring frequently, for 10 minutes or until softened and liquid evaporates.

Add spinach in batches and cook, tossing frequently, for 3 to 4 minutes or until wilted. Remove from heat and let cool slightly. Pressing with a spoon, tilt pan and drain as much liquid as possible. Transfer mushroom mixture to a large bowl. Stir in dill, feta, and nutmeg.

Unroll phyllo dough and cover with a slightly damp towel to prevent it from drying out. Brush one sheet of phyllo lightly with melted butter, and layer another sheet on top. Repeat until you have 3 layers.

Place a thin line of spinach mixture, about ⅓ cup, along the long edge of the phyllo stack. Roll phyllo tightly around filling to create a log. Coil log into a spiral and place in center of prepared baking sheet. Brush lightly with butter. Continue filling, rolling, and coiling additional phyllo logs around center spiral, building outward until all spinach mixture and phyllo are used. Brush each section with butter to hold spiral together.

Brush top of spiral generously with melted butter. Bake for 40 to 50 minutes or until phyllo is golden and crisp.

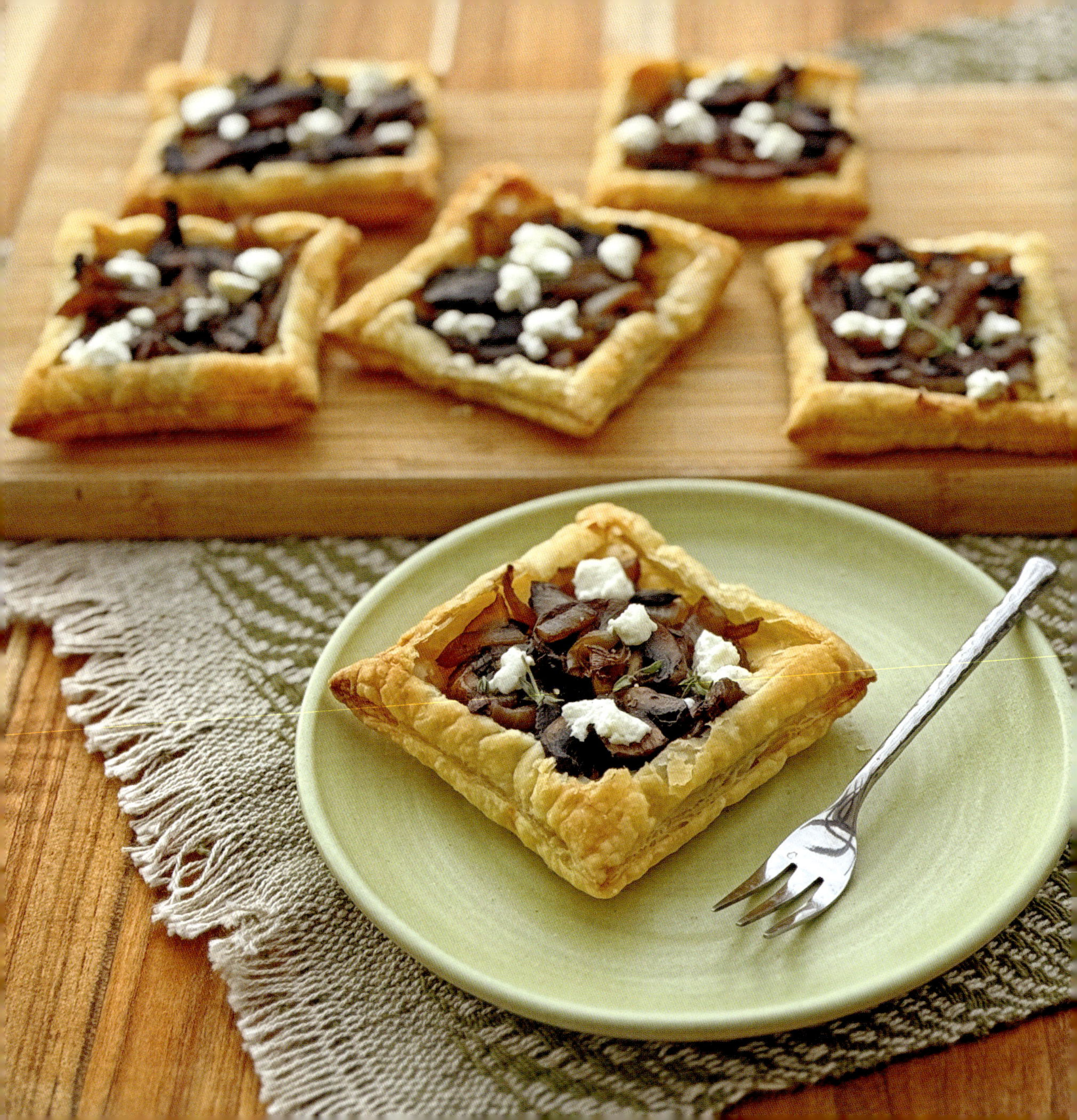

Caramelized Mushroom-and-Onion Tartlets

These small tarts are simple to prepare yet impressive,
making them ideal for every occasion, from cocktail parties to casual dinners.

INGREDIENTS

1 tablespoon extra-virgin
    olive oil
1 large sweet onion,
    halved and sliced
½ teaspoon fine sea salt
7 to 8 ounces mixed assorted
    mushrooms, sliced
1½ tablespoons balsamic vinegar
1 sheet refrigerated or frozen-
    and-thawed puff pastry
All-purpose flour
¼ cup crumbled blue, feta, or
    goat cheese
Fresh thyme leaves (optional)

Heat olive oil in a large skillet over medium heat. Add onion and salt, stirring until well blended. Cook, stirring occasionally, for 20 minutes or until tender and beginning to brown.

Stir in mushrooms and balsamic vinegar. Cook, stirring occasionally, for 15 minutes or until vegetables are tender, onions are brown, and liquid evaporates. Set aside.

Preheat oven to 400°. Line a baking sheet with parchment paper or nonstick aluminum foil.

Roll puff pastry out on a lightly floured surface to a 12x12-inch square. Cut into 9 equal portions. Score a line about ½ inch from edges to create a border on each tart. Do not cut all the way through.

Transfer to prepared baking sheet and prick centers of each tart shell with a fork. Bake for 10 minutes or until golden brown and puffed. Press down center of tart shells, if puffed up, leaving borders raised.

Spoon mushroom mixture into center of tart shells. Sprinkle with cheese and bake for 10 minutes or until heated through. Sprinkle with thyme, if desired.

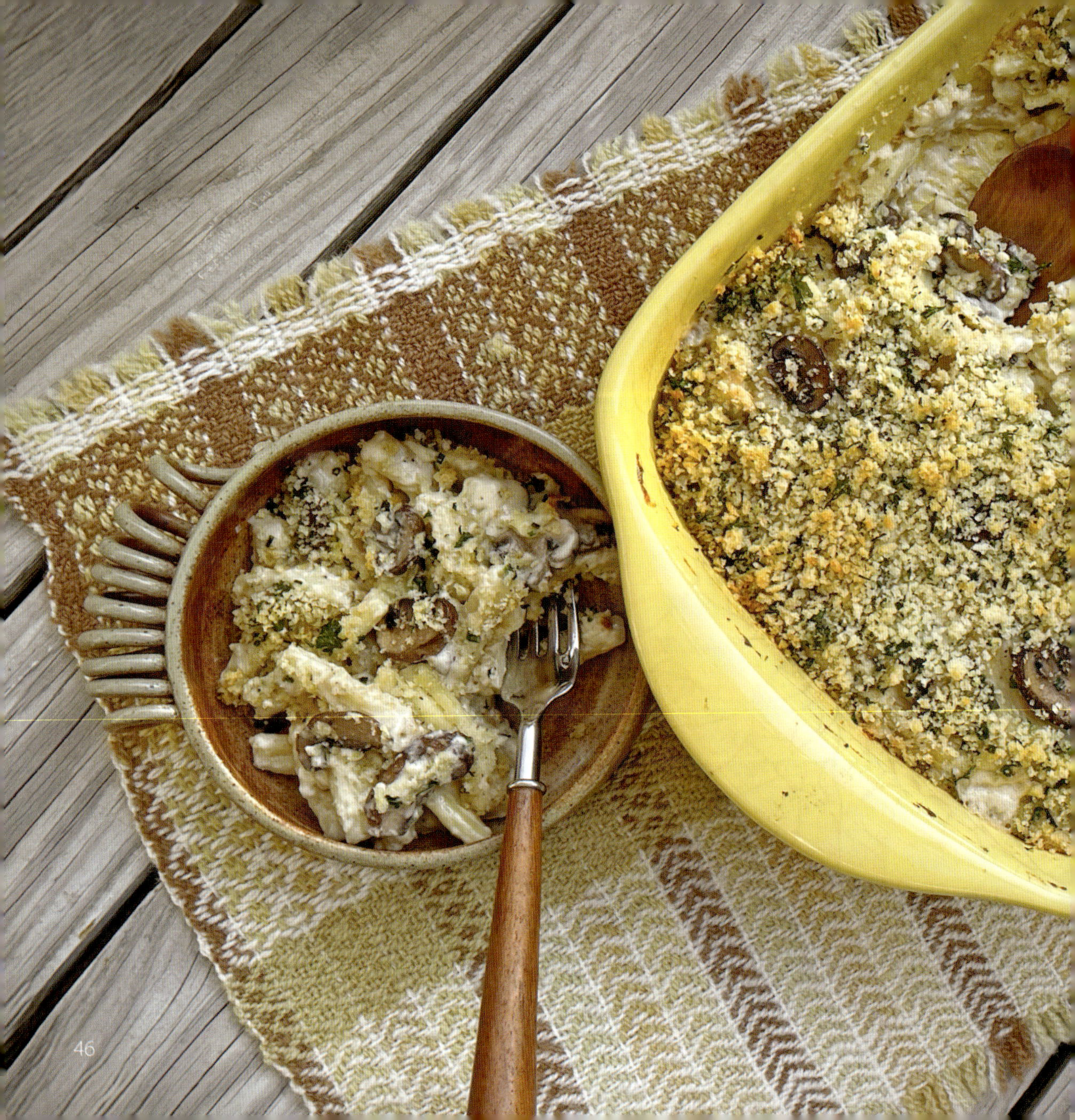

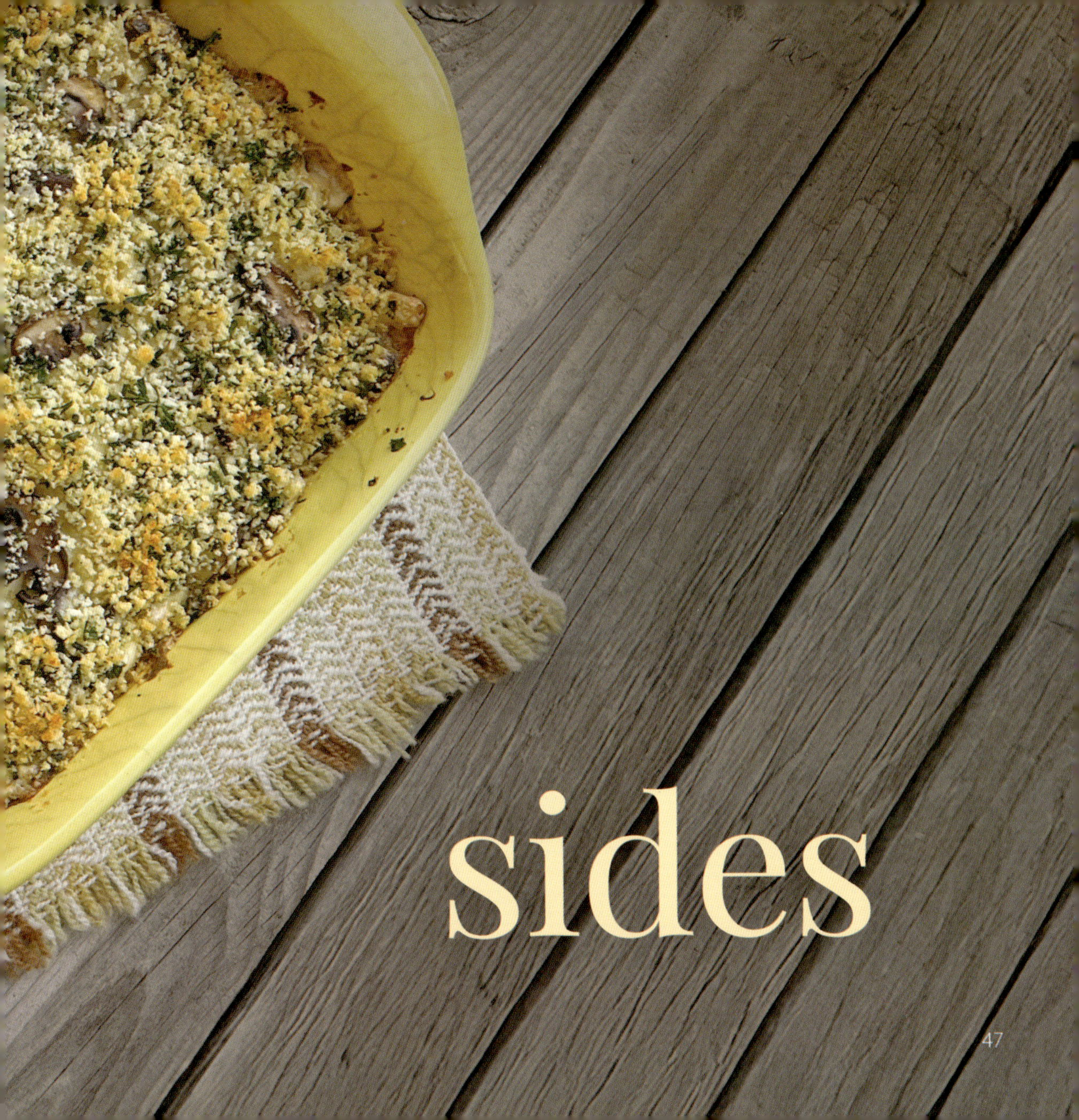

sides

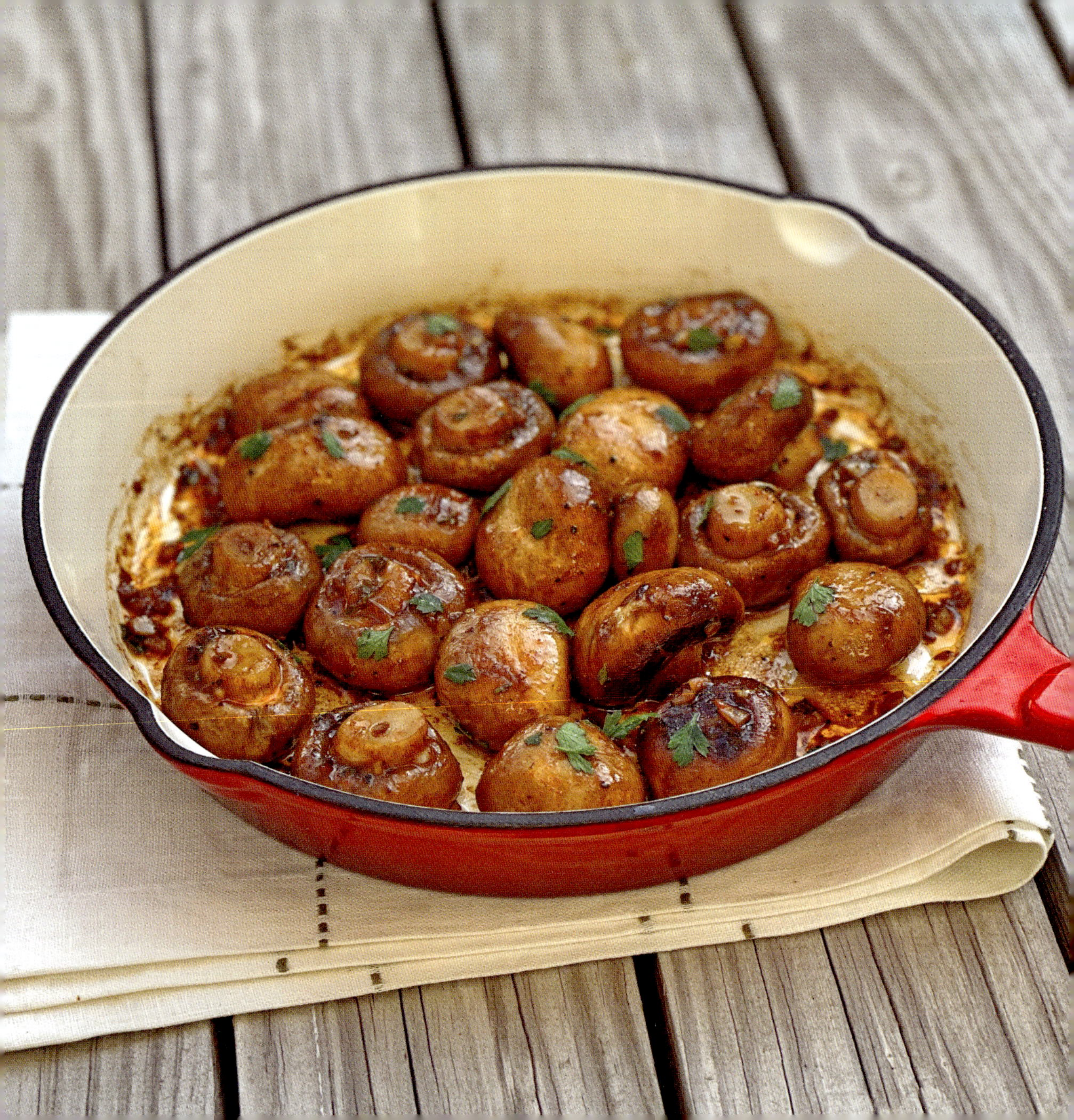

Steakhouse Mushrooms

These buttery, garlicky mushrooms cook best when they're not too large.
Look for small- to medium-size mushrooms or cut large ones into halves or quarters.
Steaming the mushrooms first in a little bit of butter helps draw out moisture.
The liquid also keeps the garlic from burning. If the liquid completely evaporates,
reduce heat even further until mushrooms are tender. Smoked paprika adds
depth to the flavor, but you can omit or substitute plain paprika.

makes 4 servings

INGREDIENTS

3 tablespoons salted butter, divided
1 tablespoon extra-virgin olive oil
1 pound or 2 (8-ounce) packages cremini or button mushrooms, stems trimmed
5 cloves garlic, minced
1 teaspoon fresh thyme leaves
½ teaspoon smoked paprika
¼ teaspoon onion powder
¼ teaspoon fine sea salt
¼ teaspoon coarsely ground black pepper
1½ tablespoons Worcestershire sauce
1 teaspoon lemon juice
½ teaspoon hot sauce
Chopped fresh parsley

Melt 1 tablespoon butter and heat oil in a large skillet over medium-high heat. Add mushrooms; cover and cook for 5 minutes.

Stir in garlic, thyme, paprika, onion powder, salt, and pepper. Reduce heat to medium and cook, uncovered and stirring occasionally, for 2 minutes. Stir in remaining 1 tablespoon butter, Worcestershire, lemon juice, and hot sauce. Cook, uncovered, for 3 minutes or until mushrooms are tender and glazed. Stir in parsley.

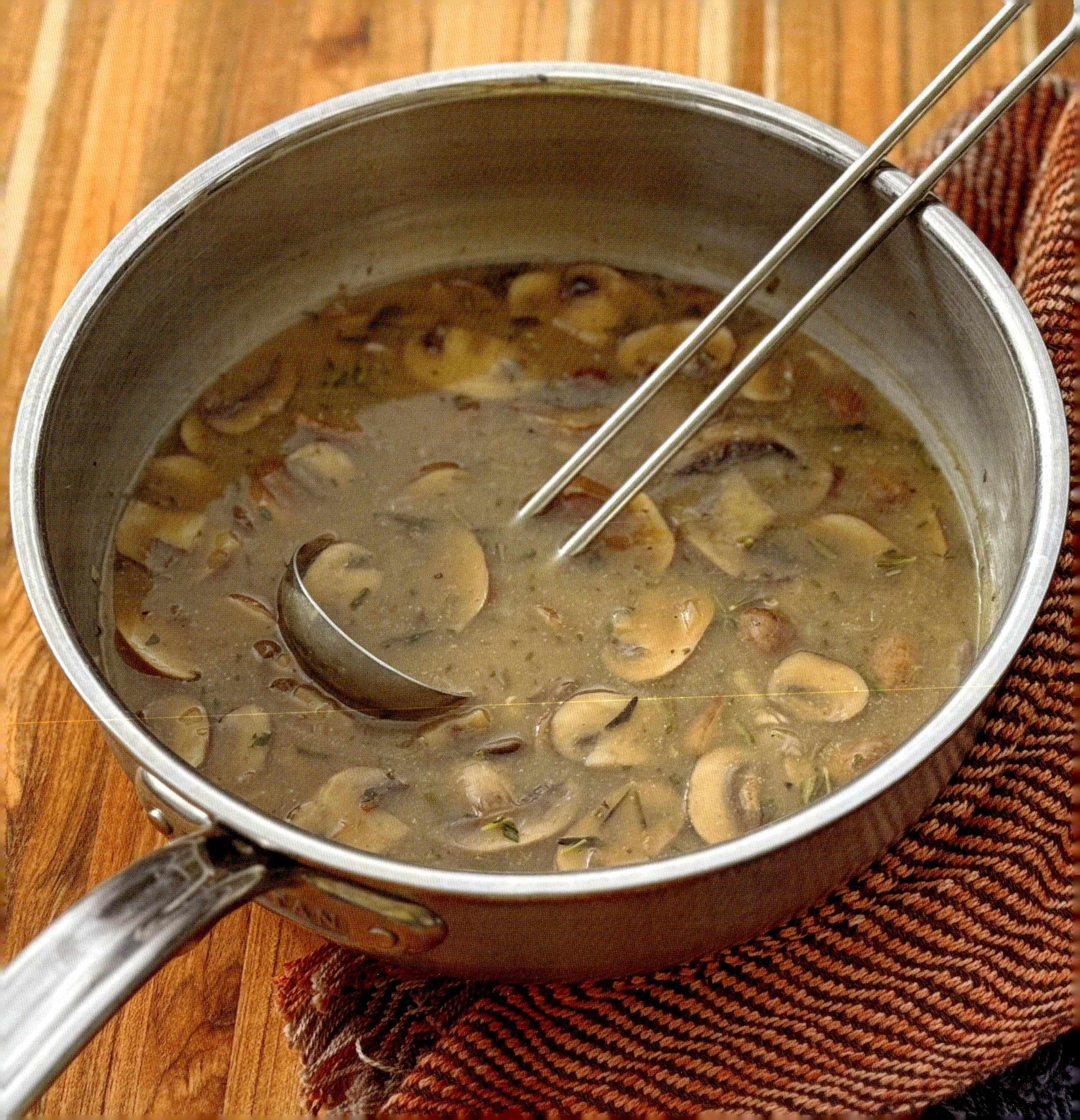

Mushroom Miso Gravy

Mushroom gravy is a rich, savory sauce that adds depth to any dish, from roasted vegetables to mashed potatoes. Made with a hearty base of sautéed mushrooms and a touch of fresh herbs, this gravy can easily be customized to suit your preferences.

makes 3 cups

INGREDIENTS

- 2 tablespoons salted or unsalted butter
- 1 shallot or small onion, finely chopped
- 1 pound cremini or another mushroom, sliced
- ¼ cup white wine
- 1 tablespoon chopped fresh rosemary
- 1½ teaspoons fresh thyme leaves
- 3 cups mushroom or vegetable broth
- 1½ tablespoons cornstarch
- 1 tablespoon white or brown miso paste or soy sauce
- ½ teaspoon coarsely ground black pepper
- ¼ teaspoon fine sea salt

Melt butter in a skillet over medium heat. Add shallot and mushrooms. Cook, stirring frequently, for 6 to 8 minutes or until mushrooms release moisture and begin to brown. Add wine and cook, stirring frequently, for 3 minutes or until wine almost evaporates. Stir in rosemary and thyme.

Spoon 3 tablespoons broth into a small bowl; whisk in cornstarch. Set aside.

Add remaining broth, miso, pepper, and salt to mushroom mixture. Bring to a boil, reduce heat, and simmer for 10 minutes.

Stir cornstarch mixture into mushroom mixture. Simmer for 3 minutes or until slightly thickened.

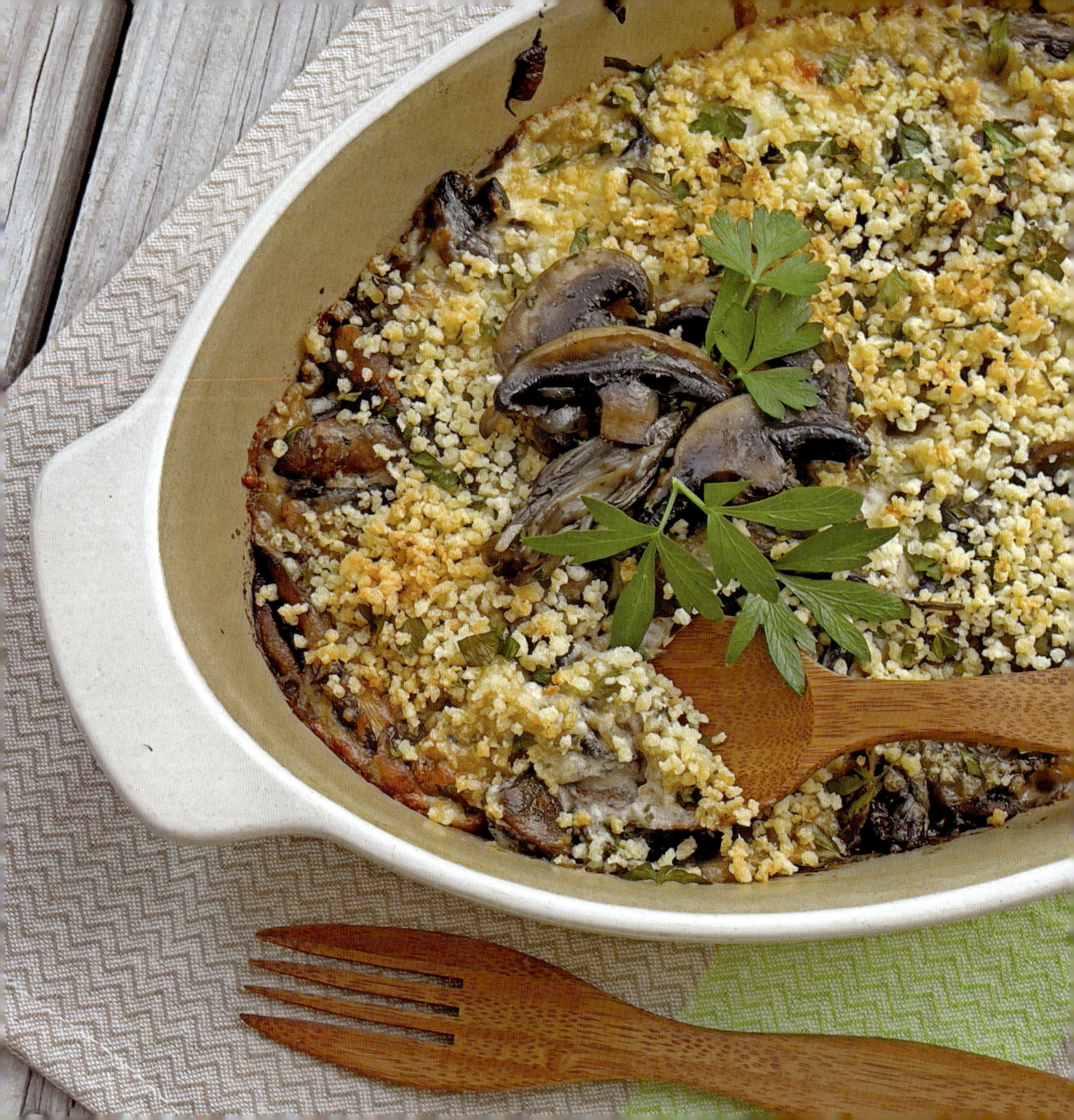

Creamy Mushroom Casserole

This side dish is creamy, cheesy, and full of rich flavors, making it a perfect side or a vegetarian main course. It's made without canned soup (which usually contains flour) and can be gluten-free or even keto-friendly if you skip the panko.

makes 4 to 6 servings

INGREDIENTS

2 tablespoons olive oil
3 tablespoons unsalted butter, divided
1 onion, finely chopped
1½ pounds fresh mushrooms (cremini, button, or a mix), sliced
2 cloves garlic, minced
2 teaspoons fresh thyme leaves
½ cup sour cream
½ cup heavy cream
½ cup (2 ounces) freshly grated Parmesan cheese
½ cup (2 ounces) shredded mozzarella cheese
¼ teaspoon paprika
¼ teaspoon fine sea salt
¼ teaspoon coarsely ground black pepper
½ cup panko or breadcrumbs
2 tablespoons chopped fresh parsley

GARNISH

Italian parsley sprigs

Preheat oven to 350°. Grease (with butter) a 1½- to 2-quart baking dish.

Heat olive oil and 2 tablespoons butter over medium heat. Add onion and cook for 4 to 5 minutes or until tender. Add mushrooms; cook for 8 to 10 minutes or until mushrooms are brown and liquid evaporates. Stir in garlic and thyme, and cook for 1 to 2 minutes.

Combine sour cream, heavy cream, Parmesan, mozzarella, paprika, salt, and pepper in a small bowl. Stir into mushroom mixture. Transfer mixture to prepared baking dish.

Melt remaining 1 tablespoon butter; stir in panko to combine. Sprinkle evenly over casserole. Bake for 20 to 25 minutes or until golden brown and bubbly. Sprinkle with parsley before serving. Garnish, if desired.

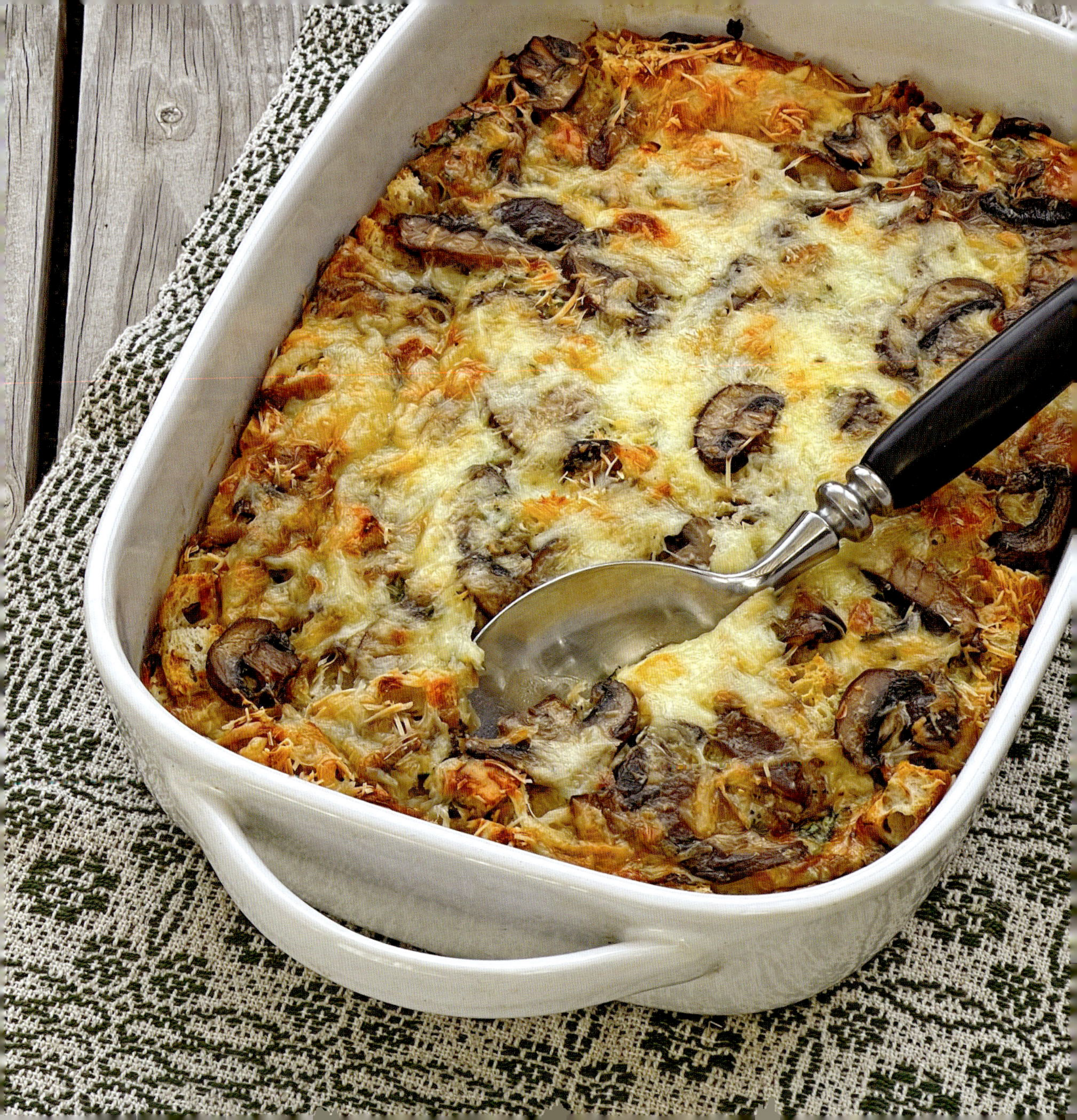

Mushroom Bread Pudding

Use a flavorful sourdough bread (such as rosemary-sea salt) for maximum flavor.
This easy-to-make-ahead dish works well as a side at brunch or dinner.

makes 8 servings

INGREDIENTS

8 cups bread cubes
  (about 12 ounces)
4 tablespoons salted butter,
  divided
½ onion, finely chopped
2 celery ribs, finely chopped
½ teaspoon fine sea salt
¼ teaspoon coarsely ground
  black pepper
1 large garlic clove, minced
8 ounces cremini or button
  mushrooms, sliced
1 (3.5-ounce) package shiitake
  or oyster mushrooms, sliced
2 tablespoons vermouth
  or sherry
6 large eggs
2½ cups half-and-half
1 cup (4 ounces) shredded
  Swiss cheese, divided
½ cup (2 ounces) freshly
  shredded Parmesan cheese,
  divided
2 tablespoons chopped
  fresh parsley

Preheat oven to 350°. Lightly grease (with butter) a 13x9-inch baking dish.

Spread bread cubes in a single layer on a baking sheet. Bake for 5 to 7 minutes or until dried but not brown. Transfer to prepared baking dish.

Melt butter in a large skillet over medium-high heat. Add onion, celery, salt, and pepper. Cook, stirring frequently, for 5 minutes or until onion is tender. Stir in garlic and mushrooms. Cook, stirring frequently, for 5 minutes or until mushrooms exude liquid and start to become tender. Stir in vermouth. Cook, stirring frequently, until liquid is reduced to a glaze. Spread evenly over bread cubes.

Beat eggs and half-and-half together in a large bowl. Stir in ½ cup Swiss cheese, ¼ cup Parmesan, and parsley. Pour over mushroom-and-bread mixture. Press down gently so bread absorbs liquid. Sprinkle with remaining ½ cup Swiss cheese and ¼ cup Parmesan. (If making ahead, cover and chill until ready to bake. Remove from refrigerator 30 minutes before baking.)

Bake, uncovered, for 30 to 35 minutes or until golden brown and set.

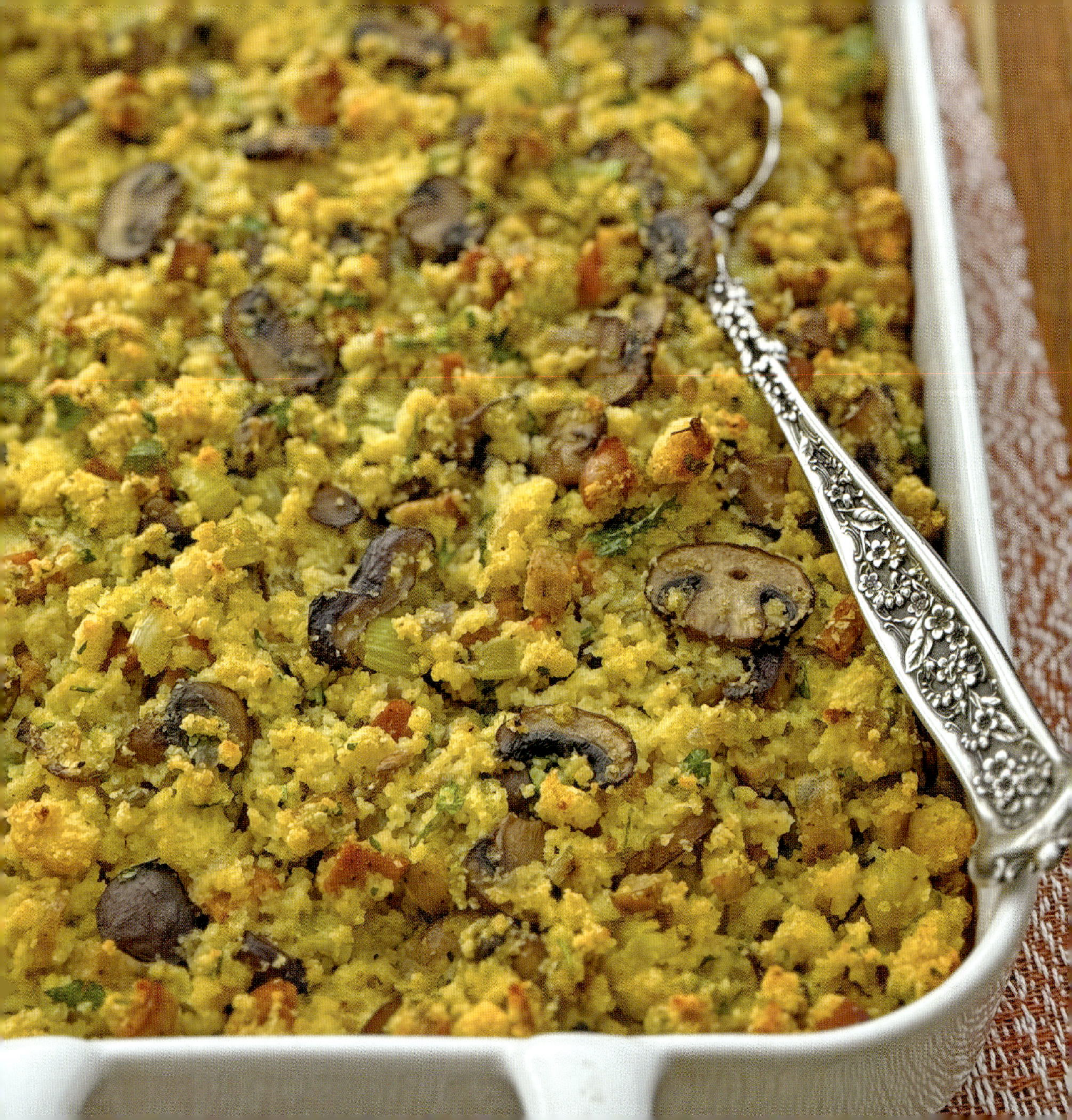

Cornbread Dressing with Mushrooms and Sausage

Aromatic herbs like sage and thyme infuse each bite, adding a recognizable, comforting flavor.

makes 10 servings

INGREDIENTS

1 pound ground mild or
   spicy sausage
7 tablespoons salted or unsalted
   butter, divided
1½ pounds assorted mushrooms
   (cremini, shiitake, or oyster),
   sliced or quartered
1 large onion, chopped
3 celery ribs, chopped
2 cloves garlic, minced
2 teaspoons fresh thyme leaves
1 recipe Cornbread,
   crumbled into small pieces
   (recipe at right)
½ cup fresh parsley, chopped
2 large eggs
3 cups chicken or
   vegetable broth
1 teaspoon fine sea salt
1 teaspoon coarsely ground
   black pepper
½ teaspoon rubbed or
   ground sage

Preheat oven to 375°. Grease a 13x9-inch dish with butter.

Cook sausage in a large skillet over medium heat until cooked. Drain; transfer to a plate. Melt 2 tablespoons butter in same skillet; add mushrooms. Cook, stirring frequently, for 8 minutes or until mushrooms begin to brown and liquid evaporates. Transfer to plate. Melt 1 tablespoon butter in skillet. Add onion, celery, garlic, and thyme; cook, stirring frequently, for 5 minutes.

Combine Cornbread, sausage, mushrooms, onion mixture, and parsley in prepared dish. Beat 2 eggs in a bowl. Stir in broth, salt, pepper, and sage. Melt remaining 4 tablespoons butter and stir into broth mixture. Pour into Cornbread mixture, stirring until well blended. Cover with aluminum foil and bake for 30 minutes. Uncover and bake for 20 minutes or until golden brown.

Cornbread: Place a 10-inch cast-iron skillet in oven and preheat to 375°. Combine **1 cup yellow cornmeal, 1 cup all-purpose flour, 1 tablespoon sugar, 1 tablespoon baking powder,** and **½ teaspoon salt** in a large bowl. Combine **1 cup buttermilk, 2 large eggs,** and **⅓ cup melted butter** in another bowl. Stir buttermilk mixture into cornmeal mixture. Place **1 tablespoon butter** in hot skillet. Pour in batter. Bake for 20 minutes or until golden.

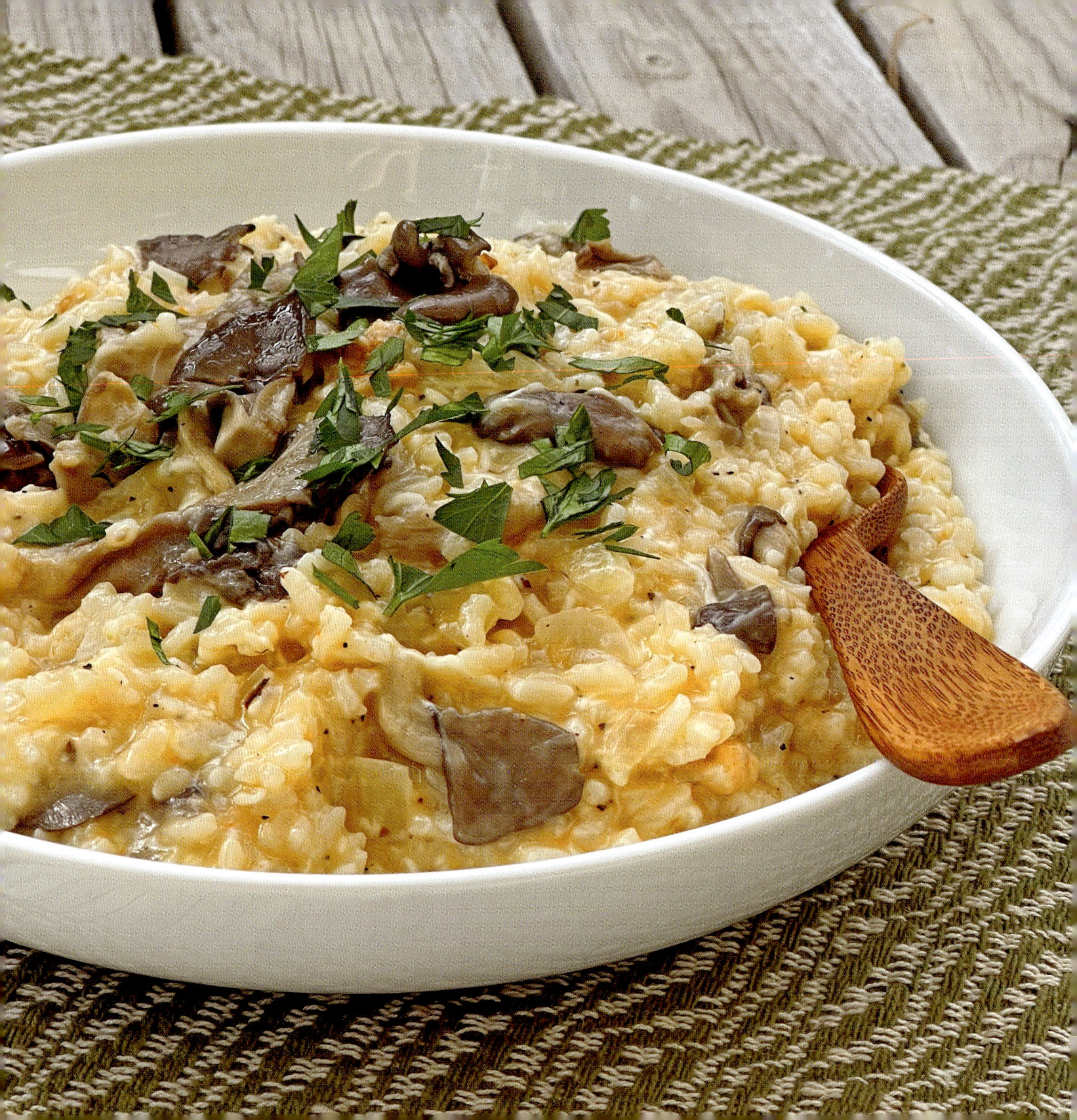

Black Oyster–Mushroom Risotto

Earthy and dark varieties of mushrooms will work well in this recipe.
Thickly slice or break mushrooms apart into bite-size pieces.

makes 3 to 4 servings

INGREDIENTS

2½ tablespoons extra-virgin olive oil, divided

8 to 10 ounces black oyster, oyster, or other mushroom, sliced into bite-size pieces

1 shallot, minced

1 cup Arborio rice

½ cup white wine

4 cups mushroom, vegetable, or chicken broth

2 tablespoons butter, cut into pieces

¾ cup (3 ounces) freshly shredded or grated Romano or Parmesan cheese

½ teaspoon fine sea salt

½ teaspoon coarsely ground black pepper

1 tablespoon chopped fresh Italian parsley

Freshly shredded or grated Romano or Parmesan cheese (optional)

Heat 1½ tablespoons oil in a large saucepan or soup pot over medium-high heat. Add mushrooms and cook, stirring frequently, for 3 minutes or until almost cooked through. Transfer mushrooms and any liquid to a bowl. Set aside a few mushrooms for garnish, if desired.

Heat remaining 1 tablespoon oil in a saucepan over medium heat. Add shallot and cook for 3 minutes or until translucent. Stir in rice. Cook, stirring constantly, for 2 minutes. Stir in wine. Cook, stirring constantly, for 1 minute or until wine evaporates.

Add about ¾ cup broth into rice and cook, stirring constantly, for 5 minutes or until broth is absorbed. Repeat several times, stirring constantly, until broth is absorbed and rice is tender yet still firm in the center (this will take 20 to 25 minutes).

Remove from heat and stir in reserved cooked mushrooms and any liquid, butter, cheese, salt, and pepper. Sprinkle with parsley and additional cheese, if desired.

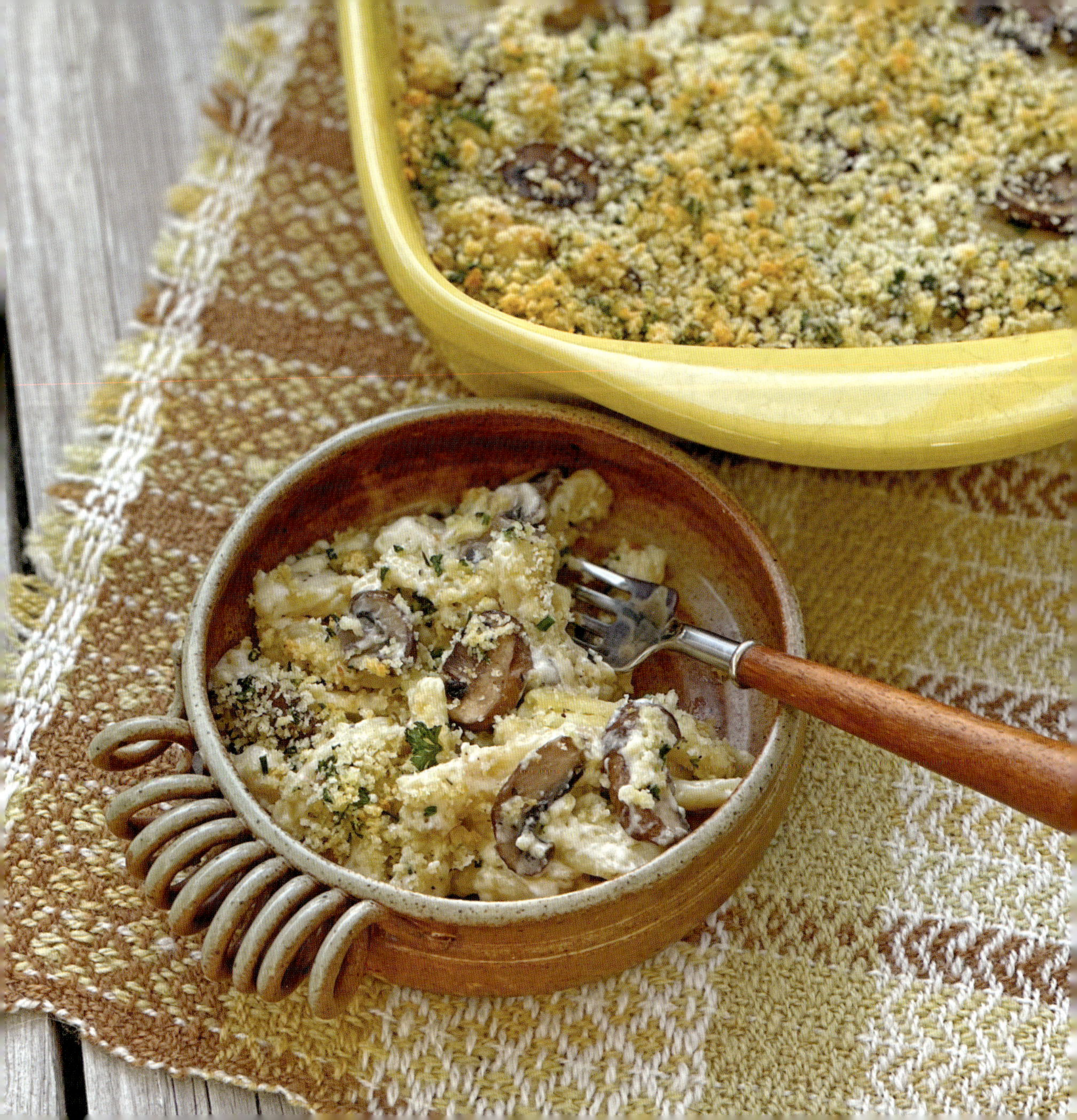

Cremini-Gouda Pasta Bake

Use a budget-friendly common button or cremini mushroom because the earthy flavor of more-expensive exotic mushrooms will be lost under the sauce and smoked Gouda.

makes 8 to 10 servings

INGREDIENTS

8 tablespoons salted or unsalted butter, divided
1 pound cremini mushrooms, coarsely chopped or sliced
2 garlic cloves, minced
1 teaspoon chopped fresh thyme
1 teaspoon fine sea salt, divided
½ teaspoon coarsely ground black pepper, divided
12 ounces uncooked gemelli, macaroni, penne, or other small pasta
3 tablespoons all-purpose flour
2¾ cups whole milk
2 cups (8 ounces) shredded smoked Gouda or Gruyère cheese
½ cup (2 ounces) freshly shredded or grated Parmesan cheese, divided
1 cup seasoned or plain panko or breadcrumbs
¼ cup chopped fresh parsley
2 tablespoons chopped fresh chives

Melt 2 tablespoons butter in a large skillet over medium-high heat. Add mushrooms, garlic, thyme, ¾ teaspoon salt, and ¼ teaspoon pepper. Cook, stirring occasionally, for 8 to 10 minutes or until mushrooms are tender and liquid evaporates. Set aside.

Preheat oven to 400°. Lightly grease (with butter) a 13x9-inch baking dish.

Cook pasta in boiling salted water according to package directions. Drain and spoon into prepared baking dish. Spoon mushroom mixture over pasta, stirring lightly.

Melt 4 tablespoons butter in a large skillet over medium heat. Whisk in flour. Cook, whisking constantly, for 1 minute. Whisk in milk. Cook, whisking frequently, for 3 minutes or until mixture begins to simmer and thicken. Stir in smoked Gouda and half of Parmesan cheese. Cook, stirring frequently, until cheese melts. Stir into pasta mixture

Melt remaining 2 tablespoons butter. Combine panko, parsley, chives, remaining ¼ teaspoon salt, and remaining ¼ teaspoon pepper in a small bowl. Add butter, stirring to coat. Sprinkle panko mixture evenly over pasta mixture.

Bake, uncovered, for 30 minutes or until golden brown.

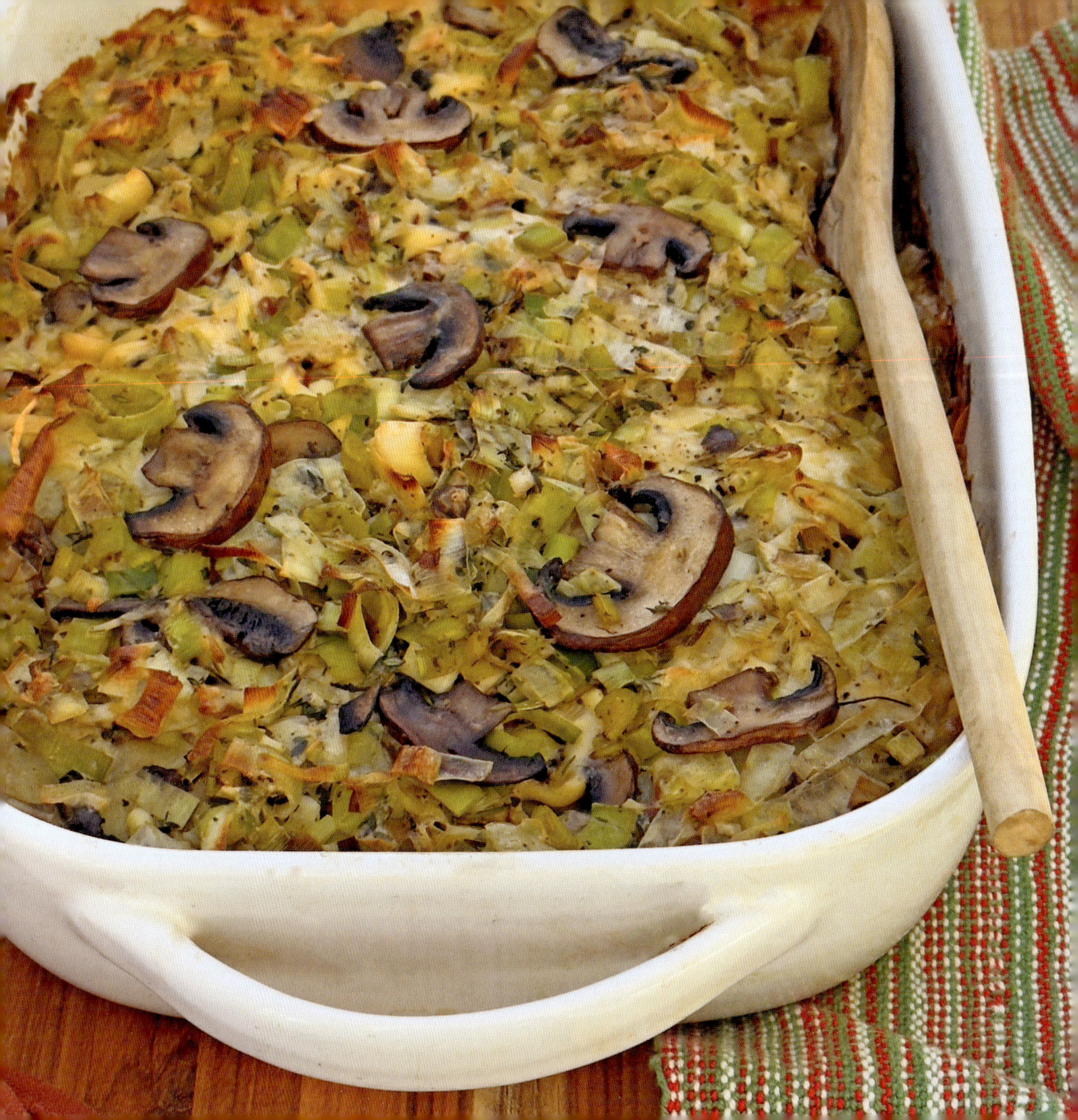

Mushroom-Potato-Leek Gratin

This dish is comforting and elegant, perfect for special occasions or cozy family dinners. Peel the potatoes or keep the skins on, whichever you prefer. Using a mandolin will make slicing the potatoes easier.

makes 8 to 10 servings

INGREDIENTS

- 2 tablespoons salted or unsalted butter
- 1 pound cremini or other mushroom, thinly sliced
- 1 leek (white and light-green parts only), thinly sliced
- 1 garlic clove, minced
- 1 tablespoon fresh thyme leaves
- 1 cup heavy cream
- 1 cup mushroom, vegetable, or chicken broth
- 1 teaspoon fine sea salt
- ½ teaspoon coarsely ground black pepper
- ¼ teaspoon ground nutmeg
- 1½ pounds Yukon Gold, yellow, or red potatoes, thinly sliced
- 1 cup (4 ounces) shredded Gruyère or Fontina cheese, divided
- ½ cup (2 ounces) freshly grated Parmesan cheese, divided

Preheat oven to 375°. Lightly grease (with butter) a 9x9-inch, 8x8-inch, or 2-quart baking dish.

Melt butter in a large skillet over medium heat. Add mushrooms and leek; cook, stirring occasionally, for 8 to 10 minutes or until mushrooms are browned and liquid evaporates. Stir in garlic and thyme; cook for 1 minute.

Combine cream, broth, salt, pepper, and nutmeg.

Layer half of potato slices in prepared baking dish, overlapping slightly. Spread half of reserved mushroom mixture over potatoes; sprinkle with half of Gruyère and half of Parmesan. Repeat with remaining half of potatoes, mushrooms, and cheeses. Pour cream mixture evenly over casserole.

Cover with aluminum foil and bake for 60 minutes or until potatoes are tender. Uncover and bake for 15 to 20 minutes or until bubbly and golden brown.

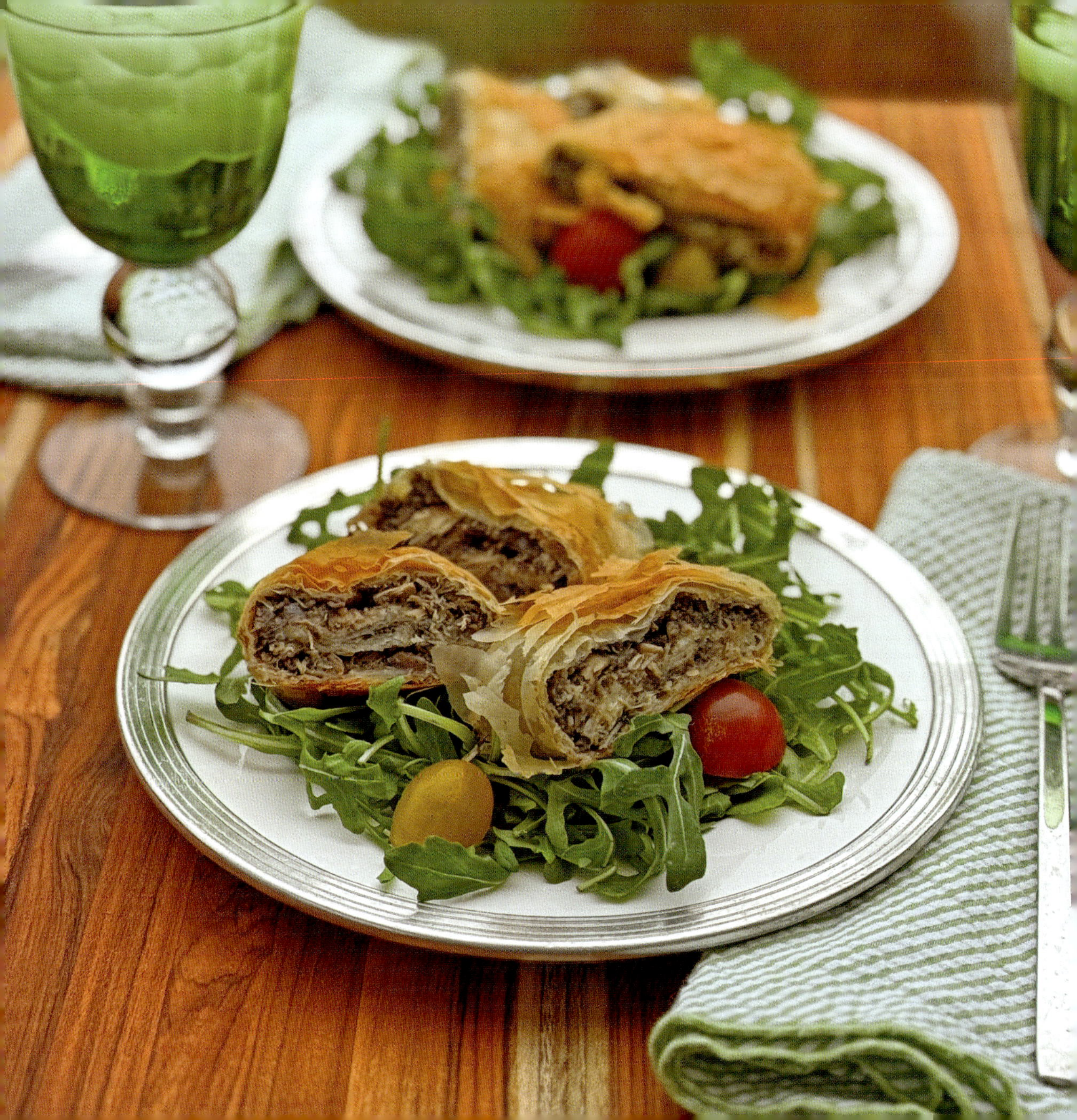

Chicken-and-Mushroom Strudel with Greens

This elegant strudel is light yet satisfying.

makes 4 servings

INGREDIENTS

8 tablespoons salted or unsalted
  butter, divided
1 tablespoon extra-virgin olive oil
1 pound assorted mushrooms
  (cremini, shiitake, oyster, or
  other), chopped
¼ red onion, finely chopped
2 cloves garlic, minced
1 teaspoon fresh (or ½ teaspoon
  dried) thyme leaves
½ teaspoon fine sea salt
¼ teaspoon coarsely ground
  black pepper
¼ cup dry white wine
2 cups chopped rotisserie or
  cooked chicken
12 sheets frozen phyllo dough,
  thawed
½ cup (2 ounces) shredded
  Swiss cheese
¼ cup (1 ounce) freshly grated
  Parmesan cheese
Arugula or other salad greens
Grape tomatoes

Preheat oven to 400°. Line a baking sheet with parchment paper.

Melt 2 tablespoons butter and olive oil in a skillet over medium heat. Add mushrooms, onion, garlic, thyme, salt, and pepper. Cook, stirring frequently, for 10 minutes or until mushrooms release moisture and begin to brown. Add wine. Cook, stirring constantly, for 2 minutes or until wine evaporates. Remove from heat and stir in chicken.

Melt remaining 6 tablespoons butter. Place 1 sheet phyllo dough on a work surface; brush lightly with melted butter. Layer with 5 additional sheets, brushing each with butter. Keep remaining phyllo covered with a damp towel.

Spoon half of mushroom mixture lengthwise down center of phyllo stack, leaving a 1-inch border. Sprinkle with half of cheeses. Roll short sides of phyllo just over filling, then roll entire bundle on the long side into a log about 3½ inches wide. Place, seam side down, on baking sheet. Brush with remaining butter. Repeat with remaining phyllo and filling to create 2 strudels.

Bake for 20 to 25 minutes or until golden brown. Let stand for 5 minutes before slicing. Serve over greens with tomatoes.

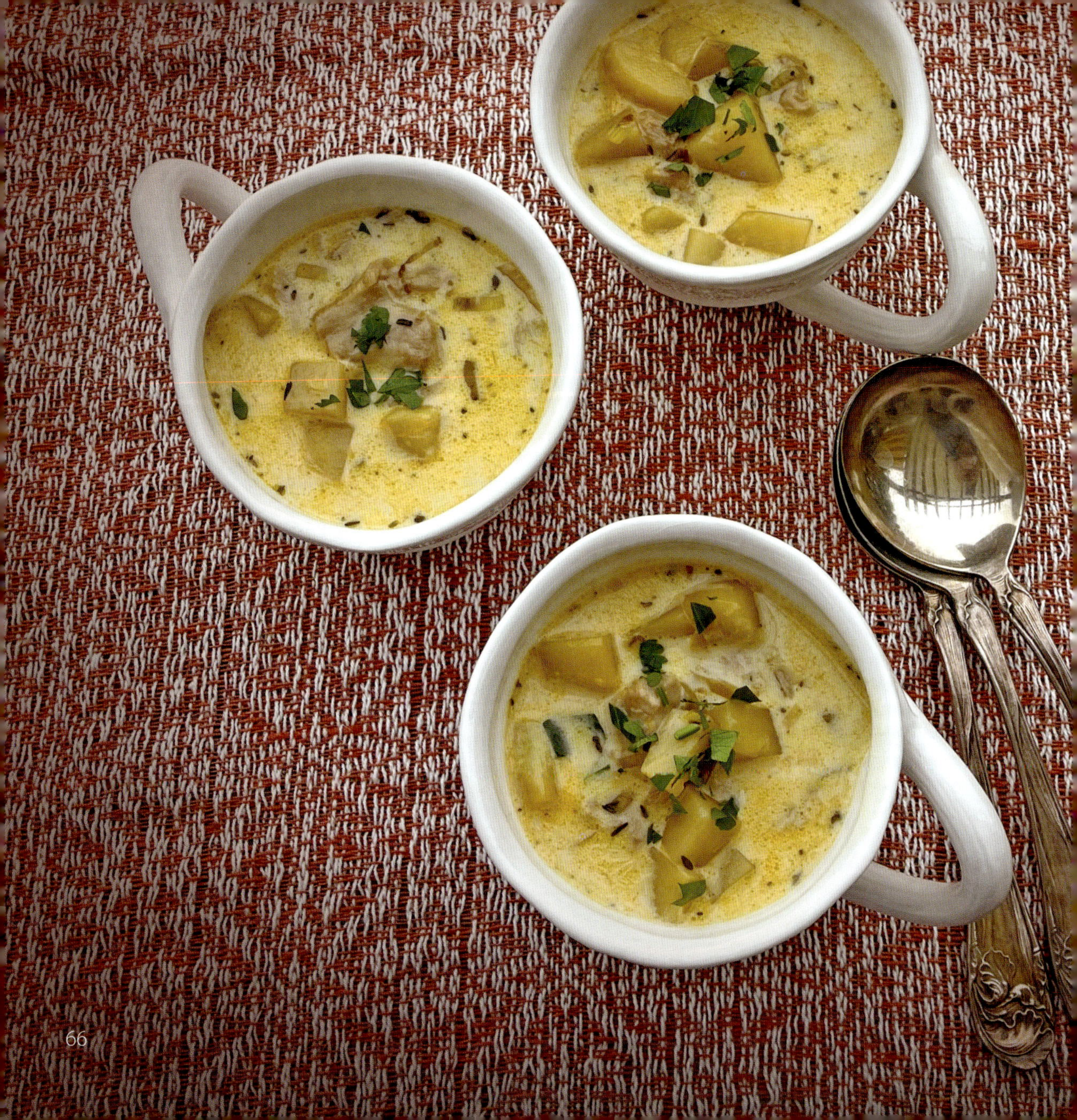

soups & stews

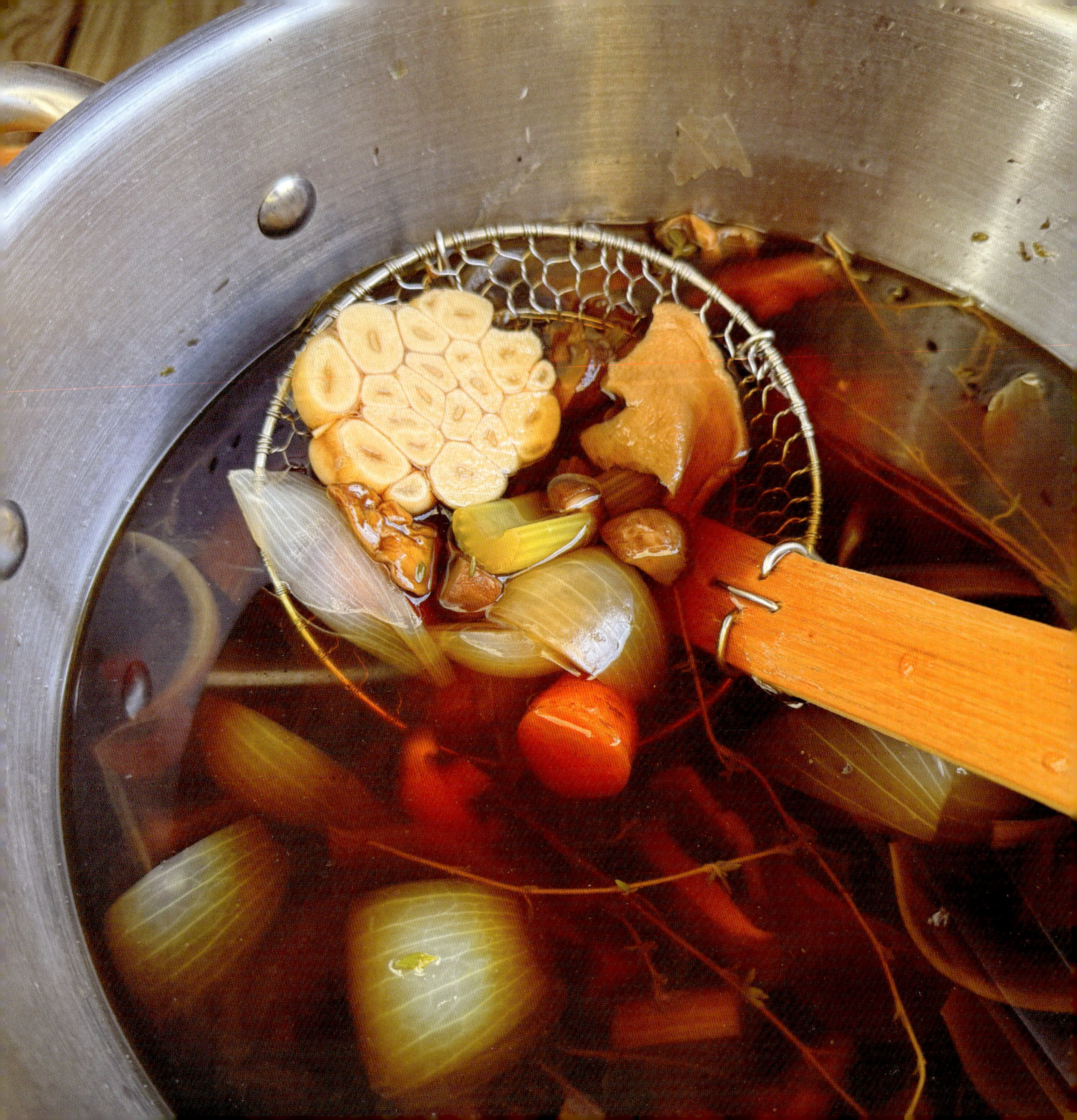

Mushroom Broth

Rich, savory, and deeply aromatic, this broth is the perfect foundation for soups, risottos, or stews. Don't let those precious porcini go to waste—after steeping, they can be chopped and added to pastas, pizzas, or sautéed dishes, making this recipe as versatile as it is flavorful. Keep this broth on hand to elevate your favorite recipes, or enjoy it as a comforting cup on its own.

makes about 7 cups

INGREDIENTS

8 cups water
½ ounce dried
    porcini mushrooms
1 pound cremini or other
    mushroom (including stems),
    coarsely chopped
1 yellow or white onion,
    cut into wedges
2 celery ribs, cut into pieces
2 carrots, cut into pieces
1 whole head garlic, papery
    exterior removed and
    halved horizontally
1 bay leaf
2 (4- to 5-inch) fresh
    thyme sprigs
½ teaspoon whole
    black peppercorns
2 tablespoons tamari or soy sauce

Place 8 cups water in a large soup pot. Stir in dried mushrooms, fresh mushrooms, onion, celery, carrots, garlic, bay leaf, thyme, peppercorns, and tamari.

Bring to a boil, reduce heat to medium low, and simmer for 45 minutes. Let cool.

Strain broth through cheesecloth or a fine wire-mesh strainer, pressing with a spoon to extract liquid. Save pieces of porcini and other mushrooms for other uses, if desired. Remove and discard bay leaf.

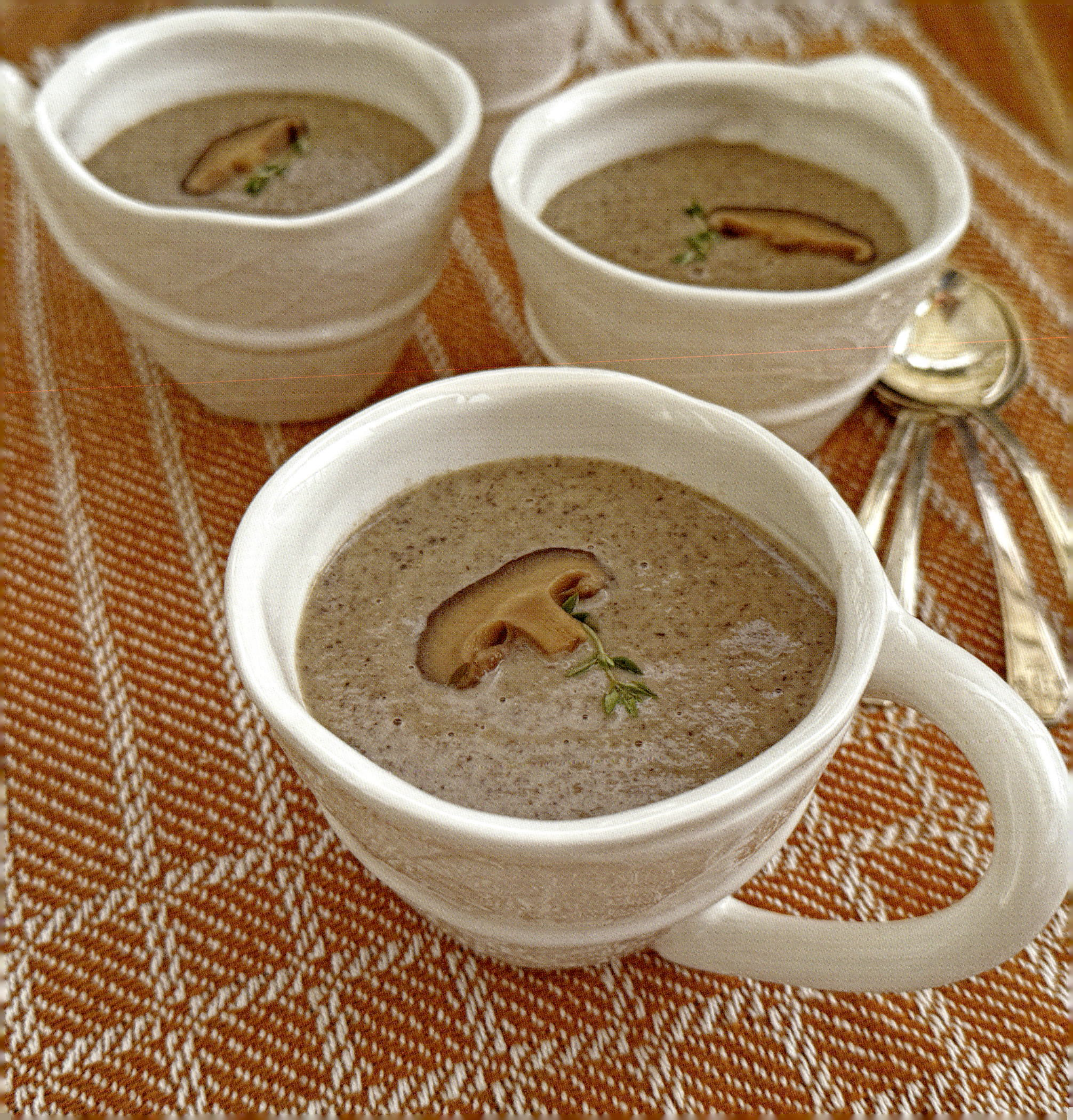

Cream of Cremini Soup

Silky, savory, and deeply satisfying, this homemade cream-of-mushroom soup elevates a humble classic into a luxurious treat. Packed with the robust flavor of cremini mushrooms and a touch of cream, it's a comforting bowl perfect for chilly evenings or as a starter for a special meal.

makes 7 cups

INGREDIENTS

4 tablespoons salted or unsalted butter
1½ pounds cremini or other mushroom, sliced or chopped
1 red onion, chopped
2 teaspoons fresh thyme leaves
1½ teaspoons fine sea salt
2 garlic cloves, minced
¼ cup all-purpose flour
¼ cup dry sherry, marsala, or white wine
3 cups mushroom, vegetable, or chicken broth
1 cup whipping cream

GARNISH

fresh thyme

Melt butter in a Dutch oven or soup pot over medium heat. Add mushrooms, onion, thyme, and salt. Cook, stirring frequently, for 10 to 12 minutes or until mushrooms are tender and liquid is mostly evaporated. Add garlic; cook for 1 minute. If desired, set aside a few pieces of cooked mushrooms for garnish.

Add flour. Cook, stirring constantly, for 2 minutes. Add sherry and cook for 1 minute or until liquid evaporates.

Stir in broth and cream. Cook over medium heat, stirring occasionally, for 5 minutes or until mixture is slightly thickened.

For a smooth texture, transfer to a blender in batches and blend. Garnish, if desired.

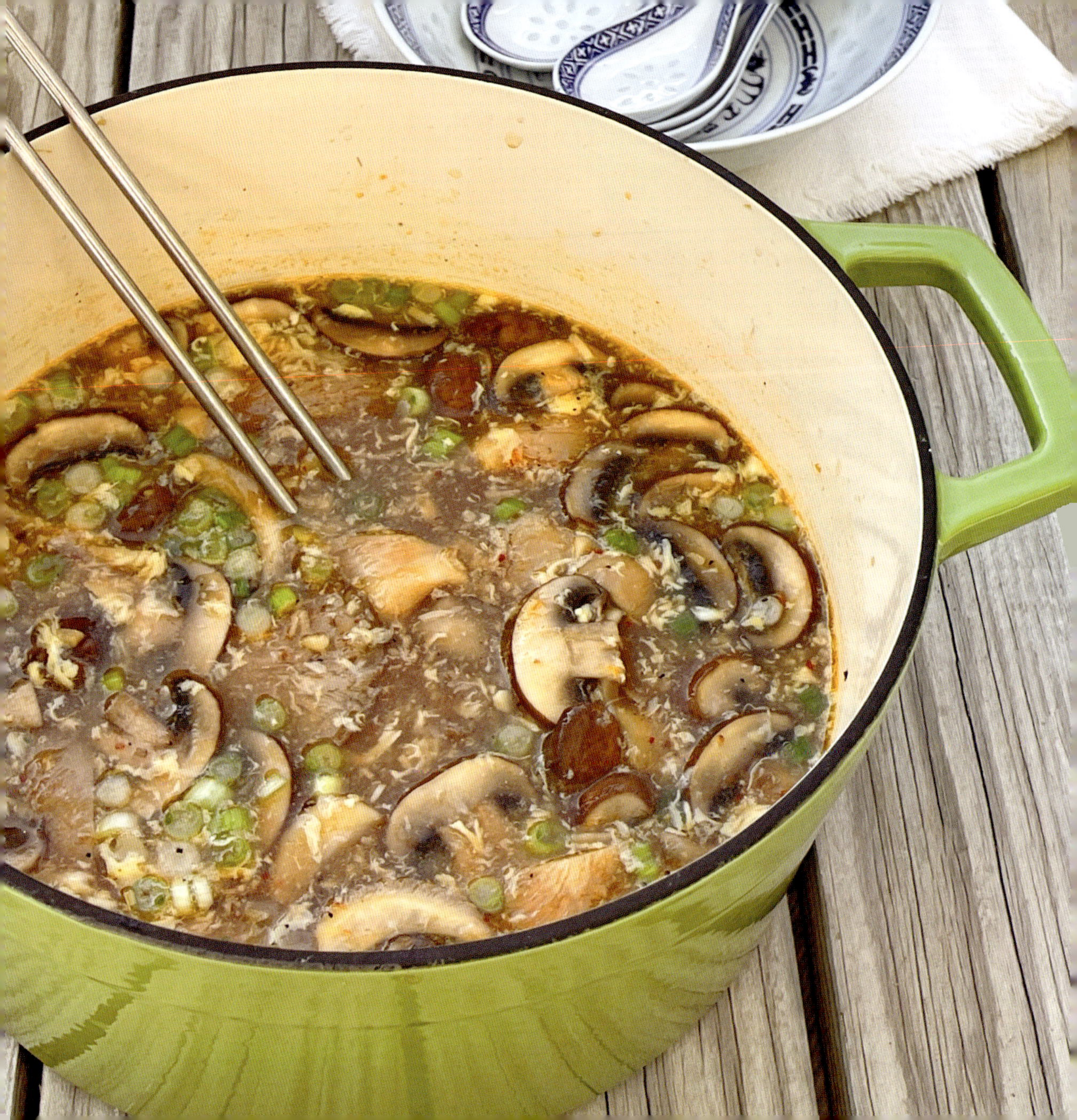

Hot-and-Sour Mushroom Soup

This well-seasoned soup balances tangy vinegar with earthy
mushrooms and tofu, creating a dish that's comforting yet zesty.
Its rich, savory broth and contrasting textures make it a favorite
for chilly days or whenever you're craving bold flavors.

makes 6 cups

INGREDIENTS

1 tablespoon avocado or
   extra-virgin olive oil
1 large garlic clove, minced
1 tablespoon grated fresh ginger
8 ounces shiitake, king oyster,
   or cremini mushrooms,
   thinly sliced
5 cups vegetable, mushroom,
   or chicken broth, divided
3 tablespoons soy or
   tamari sauce
3 tablespoons seasoned
   rice vinegar
1 to 2 teaspoons chili-garlic
   paste or sriracha sauce
½ to 1 teaspoon toasted or
   dark sesame oil
¾ teaspoon cracked
   black pepper
8 ounces cubed firm or
   baked tofu
3 tablespoons cornstarch
1 large egg, lightly whisked
3 green onions, thinly sliced

Heat oil in a Dutch oven or soup pot over medium heat. Add garlic and ginger; sauté for 30 seconds or until fragrant. Add mushrooms; cook, stirring frequently, for 3 minutes. Stir in 4½ cups broth, soy sauce, vinegar, chili paste, sesame oil, and pepper.

Bring to a gentle boil; stir in tofu.

Combine remaining ½ cup broth and cornstarch in a small bowl, stirring until smooth. Stir cornstarch mixture into soup. Simmer for 1 to 2 minutes or until mixture is slightly thickened.

Remove from heat. Add egg, stirring very slowly in one direction, creating long ribbons of cooked egg. Stir in green onions. Season with additional chili paste and/or soy sauce, if desired.

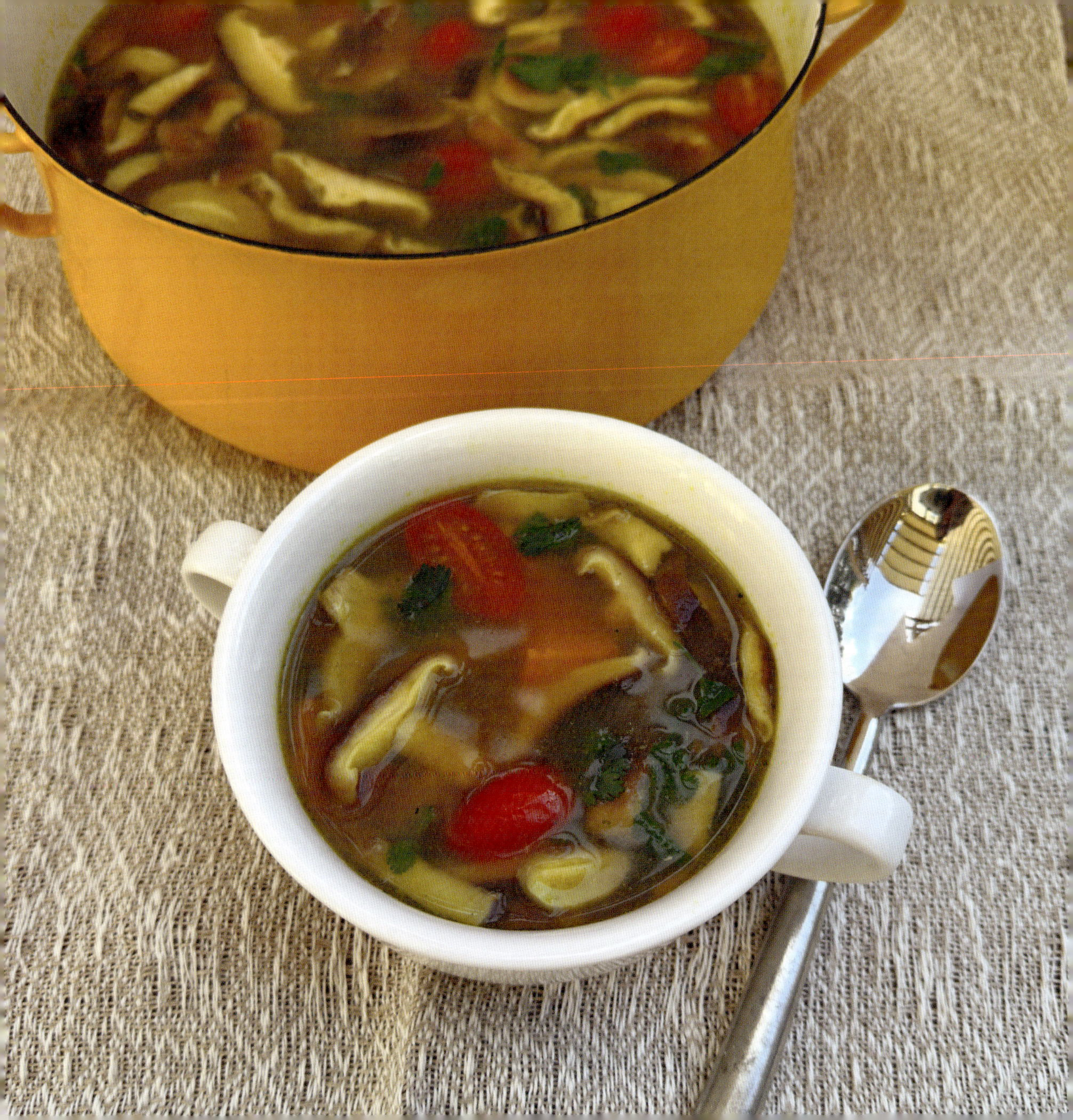

Shiitake-and-Sockeye Soup

Lemongrass and Thai lime leaves (sometimes labeled "kaffir") are found in Asian markets. In well-stocked grocery stores, you can find lemongrass paste; substitute 1 to 2 teaspoons of paste for stalks of lemongrass. For a less-spicy soup, remove seeds from jalapeño before steeping in broth.

makes 6 cups

INGREDIENTS

6 cups chicken stock or vegetable broth
4 Thai lime leaves (or 1-inch pieces of fresh lime peel)
3 (3-inch) stalks fresh lemongrass, split
5 (⅛-inch thick) slices fresh gingerroot
1 jalapeño, seeded, if desired, and thickly sliced
7 to 8 ounces shiitake or oyster mushrooms, stems removed and thinly sliced
12 ounces boneless, skinless sockeye salmon, cut into pieces
1 cup cherry or grape tomatoes, halved
2 tablespoons lime juice
2 tablespoons fish sauce
1 teaspoon light brown sugar
½ teaspoon fine sea salt
¼ teaspoon coarsely ground black pepper
¼ cup fresh cilantro, chopped

Combine stock, lime leaves, lemongrass, gingerroot, and jalapeño in a Dutch oven or soup pot over medium-high heat. Bring to a boil, reduce heat, and simmer gently for 20 minutes. Remove solids with a slotted spoon or sieve; discard.

Add mushrooms; simmer for 7 to 10 minutes or until mushrooms are tender. Stir in salmon and tomatoes. Cook for 3 minutes or until salmon is cooked through. Stir in juice, fish sauce, brown sugar, salt, and black pepper. Stir in cilantro.

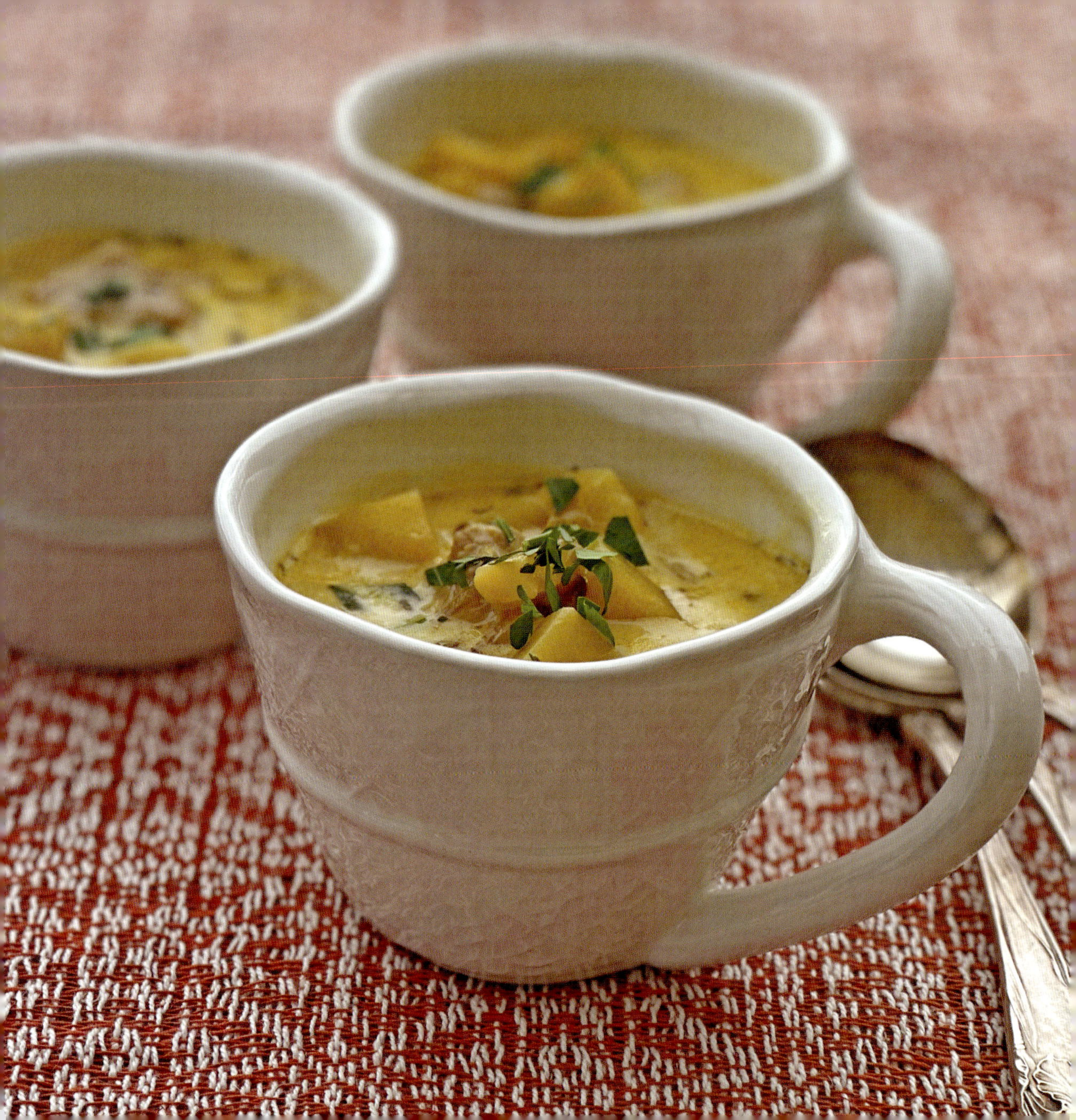

Mushroom-and-Leek Chowder

This creamy blend of tender leeks, potatoes, and lion's mane mushrooms makes a cozy, savory meal or first course. Lion's mane is a great substitution in a traditionally seafood-based soup, but you can substitute other mushrooms, ounce for ounce. Slice or chop instead of shredding. For a smoky and hardier flavor, cook 4 slices of chopped bacon and use 1 tablespoon of the drippings in place of some of the butter. Stir the bacon into the soup before serving.

makes 5 cups

INGREDIENTS

- 2 tablespoons salted or unsalted butter
- 2 medium leeks, white and light-green parts only, thinly sliced
- 8 to 10 ounces lion's mane mushrooms, trimmed and shredded into bite-size pieces
- 1 teaspoon fresh (or ½ teaspoon dried) thyme leaves
- 1 tablespoon all-purpose flour
- ⅓ cup dry vermouth or white wine
- 2 cups vegetable broth
- 12 ounces Yukon Gold or baby red potatoes, peeled and diced
- ½ teaspoon fine sea salt
- ¼ teaspoon coarsely ground black pepper
- 1 cup heavy whipping cream

Melt butter in a Dutch oven or soup pot over medium heat. Add leeks and cook, stirring frequently, for 5 to 7 minutes. Stir in mushrooms and thyme. Cook, stirring frequently, for 3 minutes.

Sprinkle in flour. Cook, stirring constantly, for 1 minute. Stir in vermouth. Cook, stirring constantly, for 30 to 60 seconds or until liquid is almost evaporated. Add broth, stirring until well blended. Stir in potatoes, salt, and pepper. Bring to a boil, reduce heat, and simmer. Partially cover and cook for 20 to 25 minutes or until potatoes are tender. Stir in cream; cook until heated through.

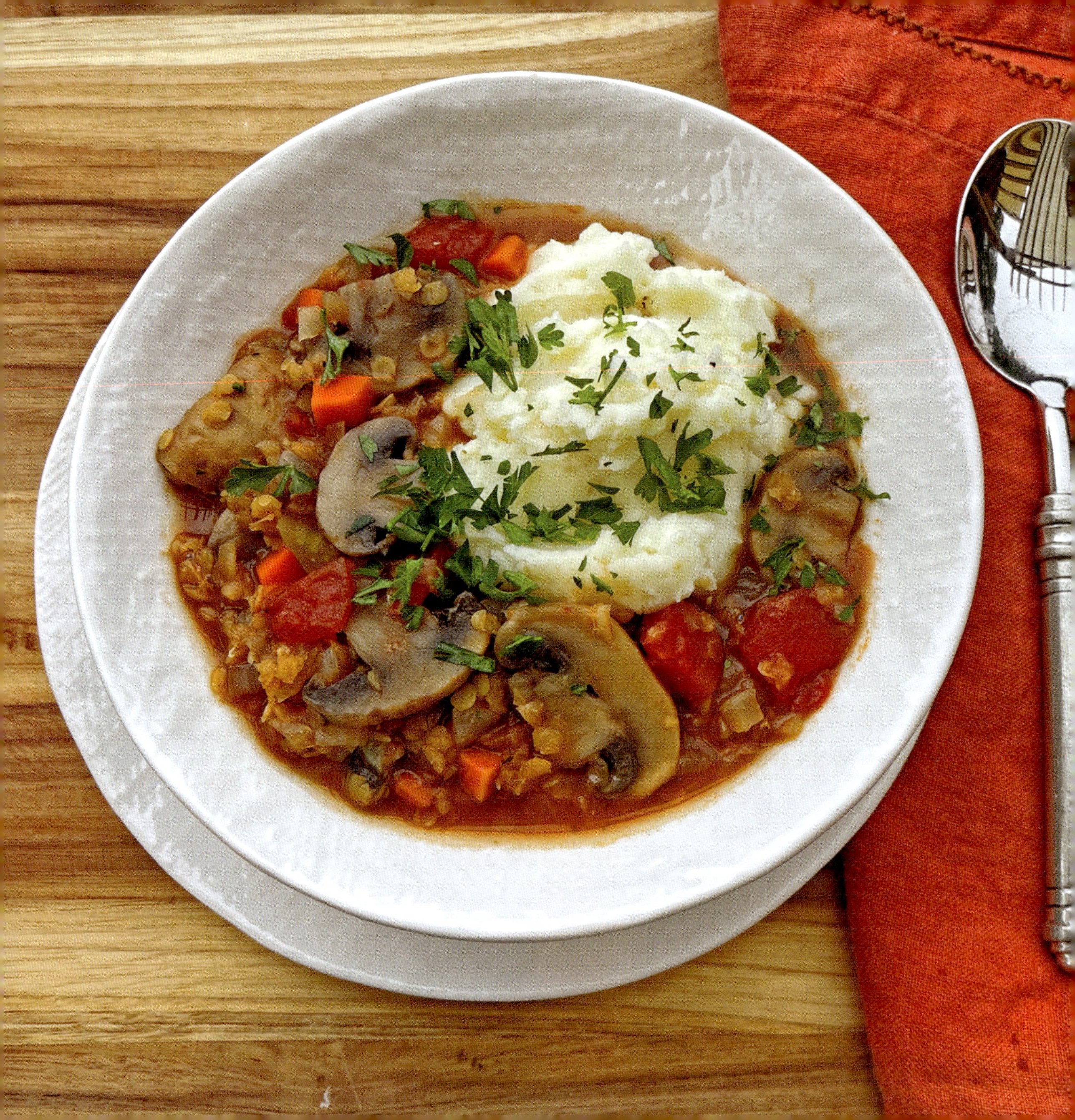

Red Lentil-and-Mushroom Stew

Cozy and nourishing, this stew is the perfect comfort food when served over creamy mashed potatoes on a chilly evening. Packed with hearty textures, it's a satisfying vegetarian meal that's easy to make and sure to please.

makes 8 cups

INGREDIENTS

2 tablespoons extra-virgin olive oil
1 large onion, finely chopped
2 garlic cloves, minced
2 celery ribs, chopped
1 large carrot, chopped
1 pound cremini, button, or other mushrooms, sliced
1½ teaspoons dried thyme
1 teaspoon ground cumin
¾ teaspoon fine sea salt
½ teaspoon smoked paprika
½ teaspoon coarsely ground black pepper
1 cup red lentils, rinsed and drained
1 (14.5-ounce) can diced tomatoes, undrained
4 cups mushroom or vegetable broth
1 bay leaf
2 tablespoons tamari or soy sauce
Mashed Potatoes (recipe at right)

GARNISH

chopped fresh parsley

Heat olive oil in a large Dutch oven or soup pot over medium heat. Add onion and cook, stirring frequently, for 5 minutes. Stir in garlic, celery, and carrot. Cook, stirring frequently, for 5 minutes or until vegetables begin to soften.

Add mushrooms and cook, stirring frequently, for 8 to 10 minutes or until mushrooms begin to brown and liquid evaporates. Stir in thyme, cumin, ¾ teaspoon salt, paprika, and ½ teaspoon pepper. Cook for 1 minute.

Stir in lentils, tomatoes, broth, and bay leaf. Bring to a boil, reduce heat, and simmer over medium-low heat, uncovered, for 25 to 30 minutes or until lentils are tender and stew is thickened. Stir in tamari sauce. Remove and discard bay leaf.

Spoon Mashed Potatoes into bowls or onto plates. Ladle stew over potatoes and garnish, if desired.

Mashed Potatoes: Place **2 pounds peeled-and-cubed Yukon Gold or gold potatoes** in a large pot with water to cover. Stir in **1 teaspoon kosher salt.** Bring to a boil, reduce heat, and simmer for 15 to 20 minutes or until potatoes are tender. Drain and return to pot. Add **4 tablespoons salted or unsalted butter, ½ cup heavy whipping cream or whole milk, ½ teaspoon fine sea salt,** and **¼ teaspoon coarsely ground black pepper.** Mash until smooth. Makes 4 cups.

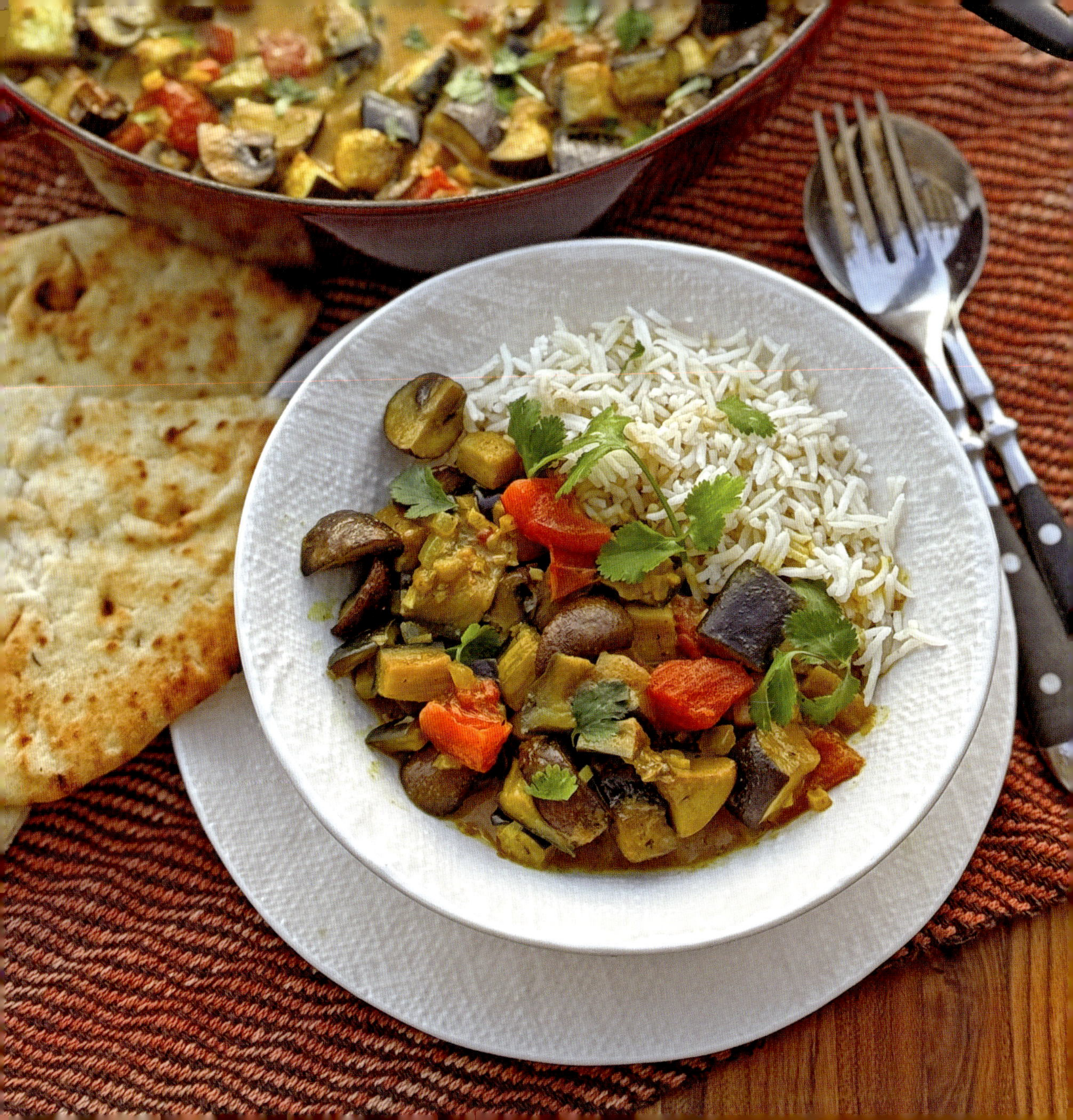

Roasted Eggplant-and-Mushroom Curry

This roasted curry is a hearty, flavorful dish that's perfect for cozy evenings. The sauce is infused with aromatic spices like cumin, coriander, and turmeric, creating a vibrant, comforting curry.

makes 6 servings

INGREDIENTS

1 eggplant, diced
1 pound cremini, button, or another mushroom, quartered
5 tablespoons extra-virgin olive oil, divided
1 teaspoon fine sea salt
1 teaspoon coarsely ground black pepper
½ onion, chopped
1½ tablespoons finely chopped fresh ginger
3 large garlic cloves, minced
1 tablespoon ground cumin
2 teaspoons ground coriander
1 teaspoon ground turmeric
1 teaspoon paprika
¼ to ½ teaspoon cayenne pepper
1 (14.5-ounce) can diced tomatoes, drained
1 (13.5-ounce) can coconut milk
¼ cup chopped fresh cilantro
Hot cooked basmati rice

Preheat oven to 400°.

Combine eggplant and mushrooms in a large bowl. Drizzle in 3 tablespoons olive oil, salt, and black pepper; toss to coat. Transfer to a large, rimmed baking sheet, spreading vegetables out in a single layer. Roast for 20 minutes, stirring occasionally.

Heat remaining 2 tablespoons oil in a brasier or large, deep skillet. Add onion, ginger, and garlic. Cook for 3 minutes, stirring frequently. Stir in cumin, coriander, turmeric, paprika, and cayenne pepper. Cook for 1 minute.

Stir in tomatoes and coconut milk. Drain vegetables, discarding liquid, and stir into tomato mixture. Bring mixture to a boil, reduce heat, and simmer for 20 minutes.

Stir in cilantro. Serve over hot cooked rice.

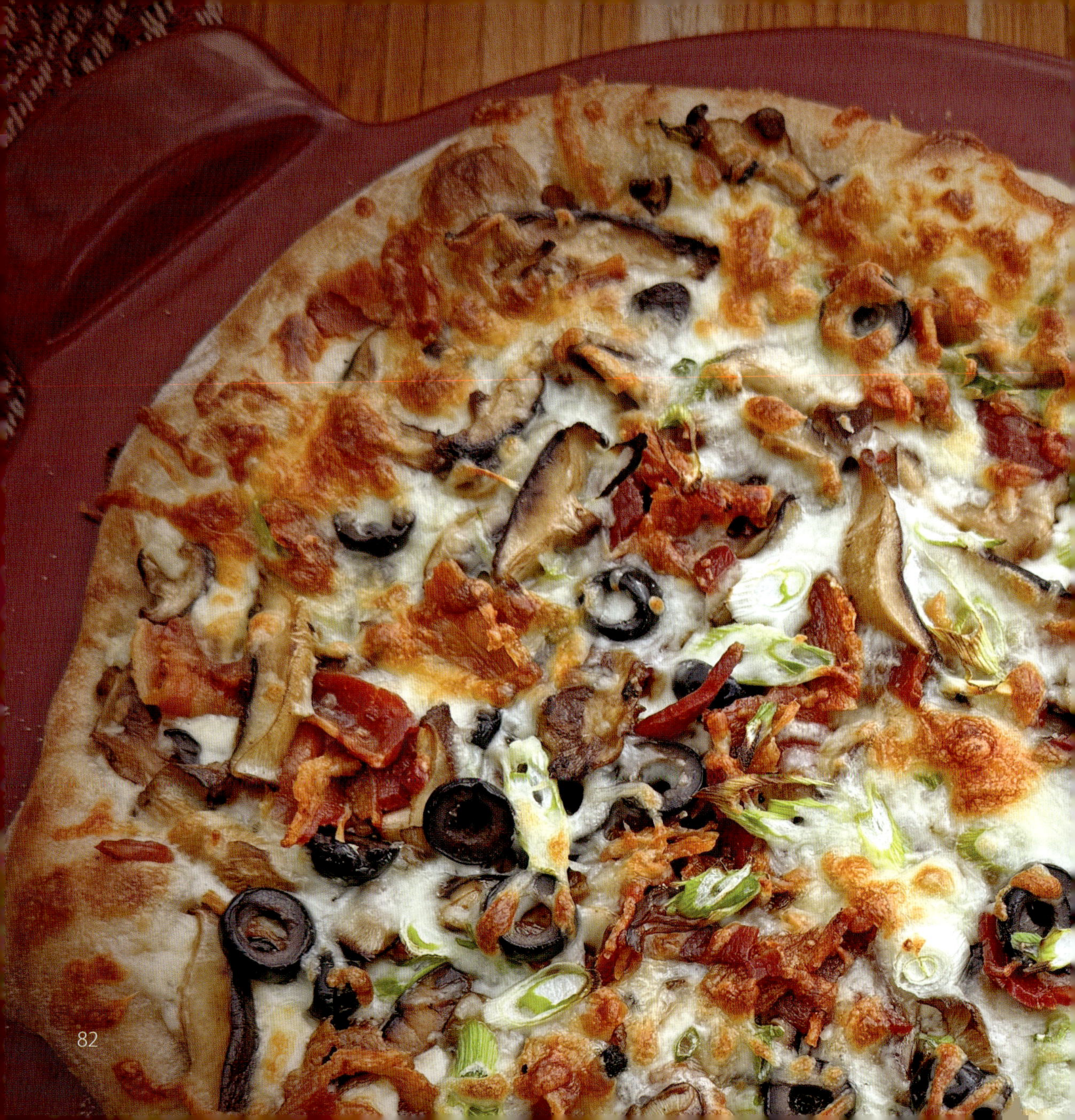

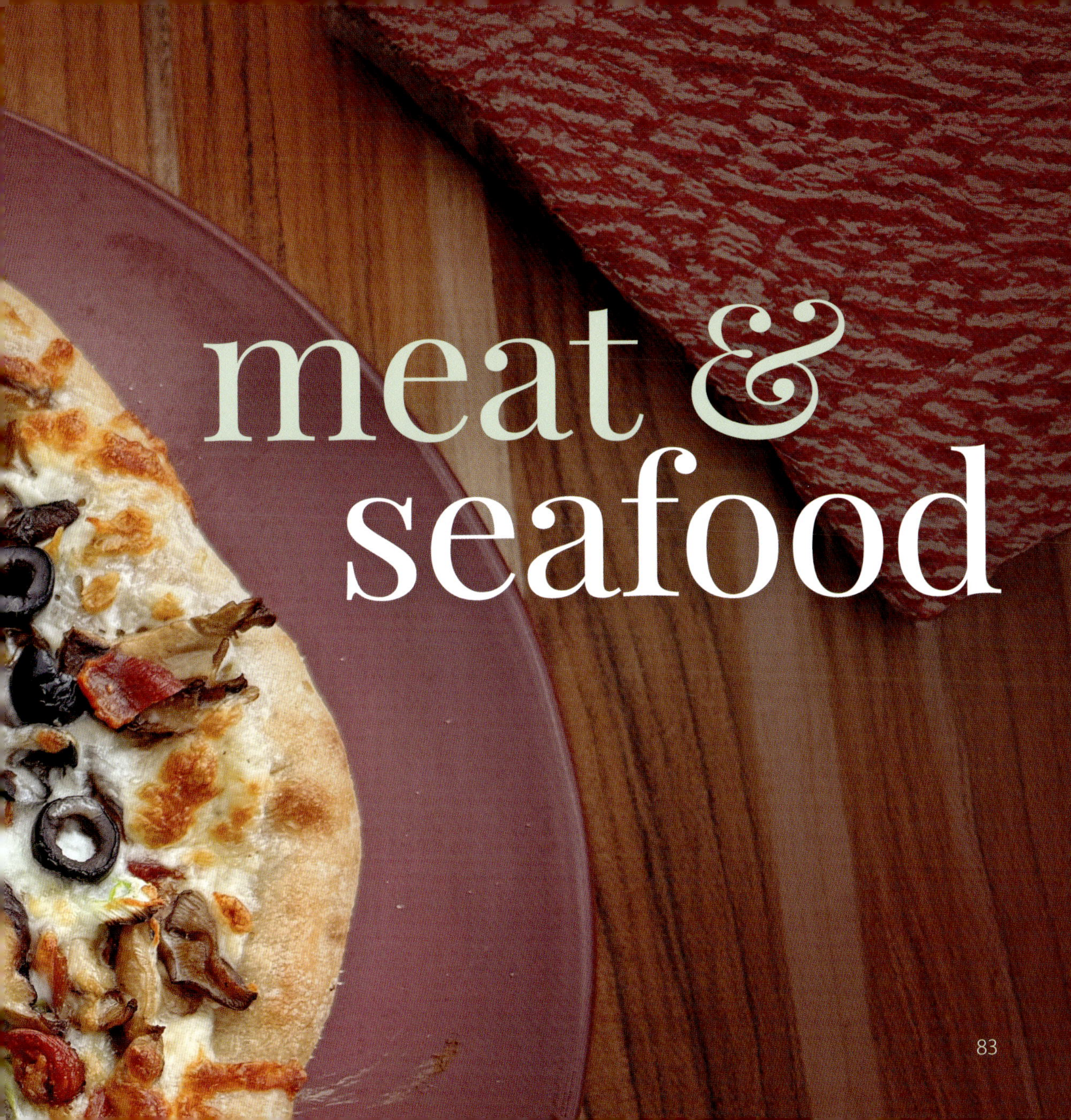

meat &
seafood

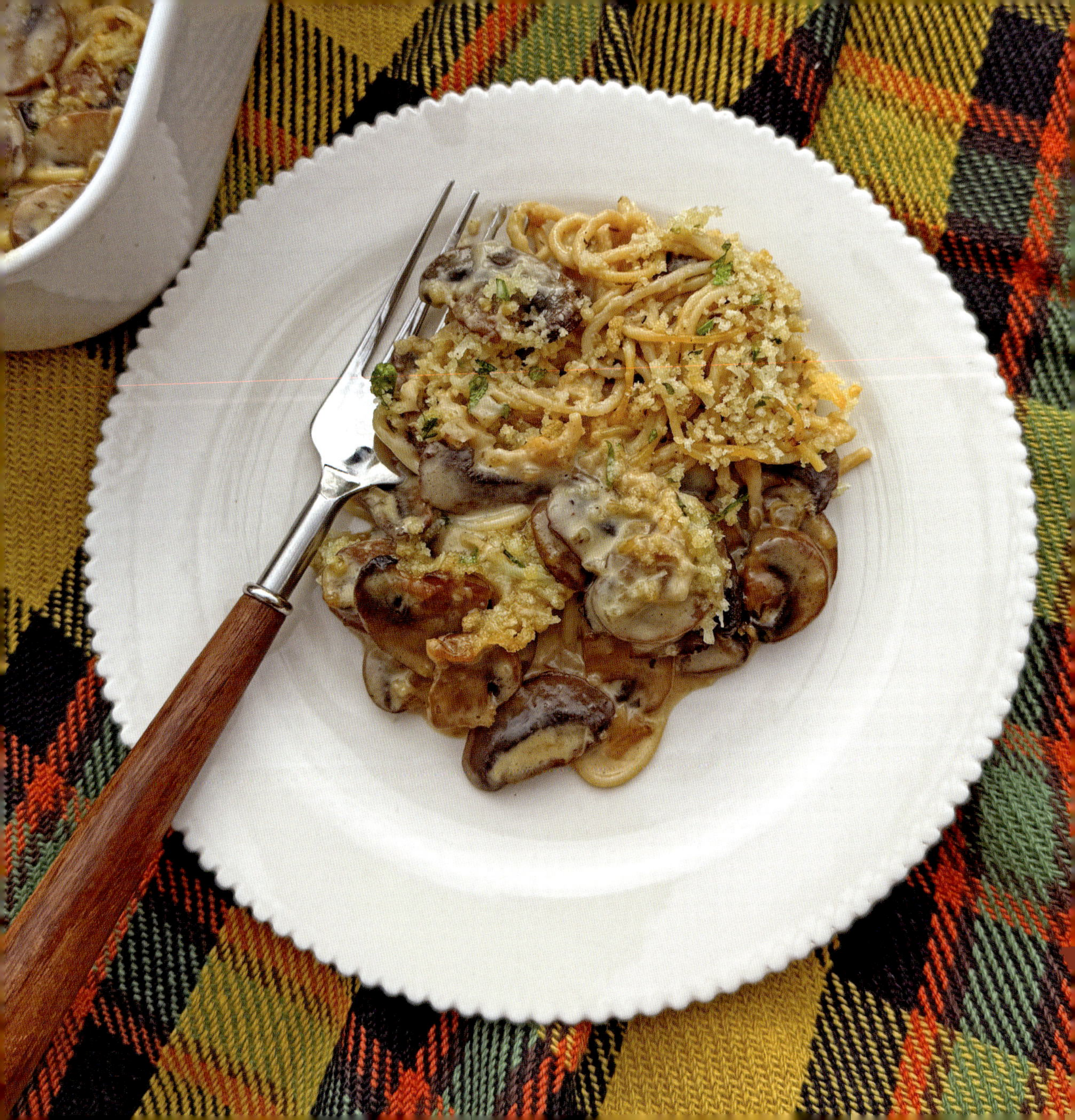

Chicken–Mushroom Tetrazzini

Comfort food meets elegance in this creamy, cheesy dish. Packed with tender chicken, earthy mushrooms, and spaghetti coated in a luscious sauce, it's perfect for a family dinner or a potluck gathering. This recipe uses just a hint of nutmeg to round out the flavors. Make it ahead for easy entertaining or serve it fresh from the oven for a cozy, satisfying meal everyone will love.

makes 6 servings

INGREDIENTS

1 tablespoon extra-virgin olive oil

7 tablespoons unsalted or salted butter, divided

1½ pounds cremini or other mushrooms, sliced

1 teaspoon Italian seasoning blend

1 small onion, chopped

4 garlic cloves, minced

½ cup white wine

¼ cup all-purpose flour

2 cups chicken broth

2 cups heavy whipping cream

1 teaspoon fine sea salt

½ teaspoon coarsely ground black pepper

½ teaspoon ground nutmeg

2 cups chopped or shredded cooked chicken

12 ounces uncooked spaghetti

¾ cup plain or seasoned panko or breadcrumbs

½ cup (2 ounces) freshly grated Parmesan cheese

1 tablespoon chopped fresh parsley

Preheat oven to 375°. Lightly grease (with butter) a 13x9-inch baking dish.

Heat olive oil and 1 tablespoon butter in a large skillet over medium heat. Add mushrooms and Italian seasoning. Cook, stirring frequently, for 7 minutes or until almost tender. Add onion and garlic. Cook, stirring frequently, for 3 to 5 minutes or until mushrooms are tender and begin to brown. Stir in wine. Cook, stirring constantly, for 2 minutes or until wine evaporates. Transfer mushroom mixture to a large bowl; set aside.

Melt 4 tablespoons butter in same skillet over medium heat (no need to wipe clean). Add flour and cook for 1 minute. Whisk in broth, cream, salt, pepper, and nutmeg, stirring until smooth. Cook over medium heat for 5 minutes or until thickened. Stir in chicken. Set aside.

Cook spaghetti according to package directions; drain. Transfer to prepared dish and stir in mushroom and chicken mixtures.

Melt remaining 2 tablespoons butter and place in a medium bowl; add panko, Parmesan, and parsley, stirring until well blended. Sprinkle panko mixture over casserole. Bake for 20 to 25 minutes or until golden brown and bubbly.

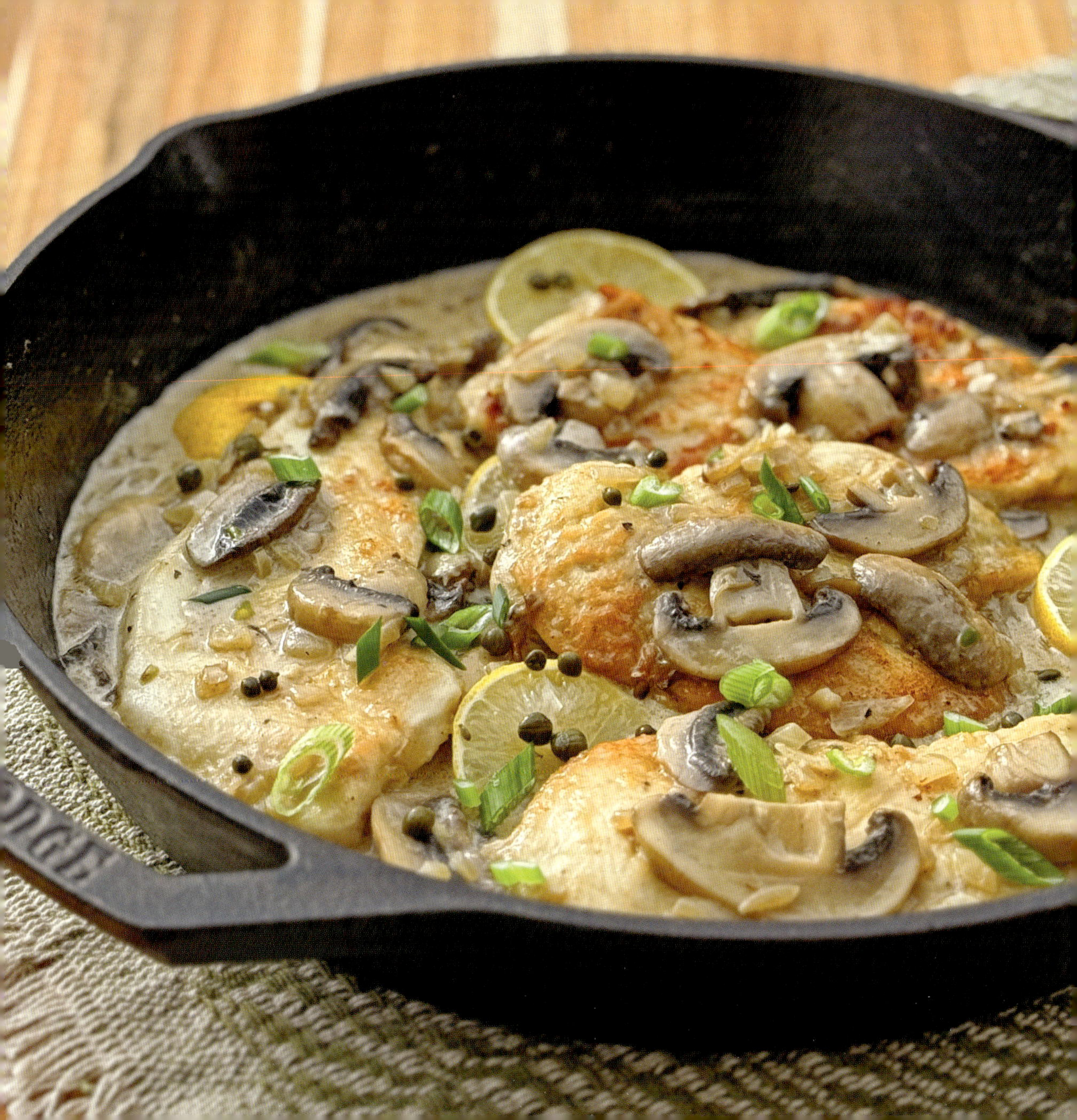

Lemon Chicken Scallopini with Mushrooms

Try this flavorful dish for weeknights or casual entertaining.
Tender chicken cutlets are lightly browned and simmered in a simple sauce
with plenty of mushrooms for added depth and heartiness. For an extra-tangy
twist, toss in some capers. Serve it on its own or over pasta or rice.

makes 2 to 4 servings

INGREDIENTS

¼ cup all-purpose flour
¼ teaspoon fine sea salt
¼ teaspoon coarsely ground
  black pepper
2 large chicken breasts
2 tablespoons salted or unsalted
  butter, divided
1 tablespoon extra-virgin olive oil
1 pound button, cremini, or
  other mushrooms, sliced
1 small onion, chopped
1 garlic clove, minced
1 lemon, sliced
¼ cup wine white
½ cup chicken broth
⅓ cup heavy whipping cream
1 teaspoon capers, drained
  (optional)

Combine flour, salt, and pepper in a shallow bowl.

Slice chicken breasts in half to create 4 thin cutlets. Flatten with a meat pounder to an even ¼-inch thickness. Dredge chicken in flour mixture; set aside.

Heat 1 tablespoon butter and oil in an extra-large skillet over medium-high heat. Add chicken and cook for 2 minutes on each side or until golden brown. Transfer to a plate; cover with aluminum foil to keep warm.

Melt remaining 1 tablespoon butter in skillet (no need to wipe clean). Add mushrooms and onion. Cook, stirring frequently, for 3 to 5 minutes or until tender. Add garlic and lemon slices, and cook for 1 minute.

Stir in wine. Cook for 2 minutes or until wine evaporates. Stir in broth. Cook for 2 to 3 minutes or until slightly thickened. Stir in cream. Return chicken to skillet and cook for 2 minutes or until sauce is thickened and chicken is cooked through and hot. Sprinkle with capers, if desired.

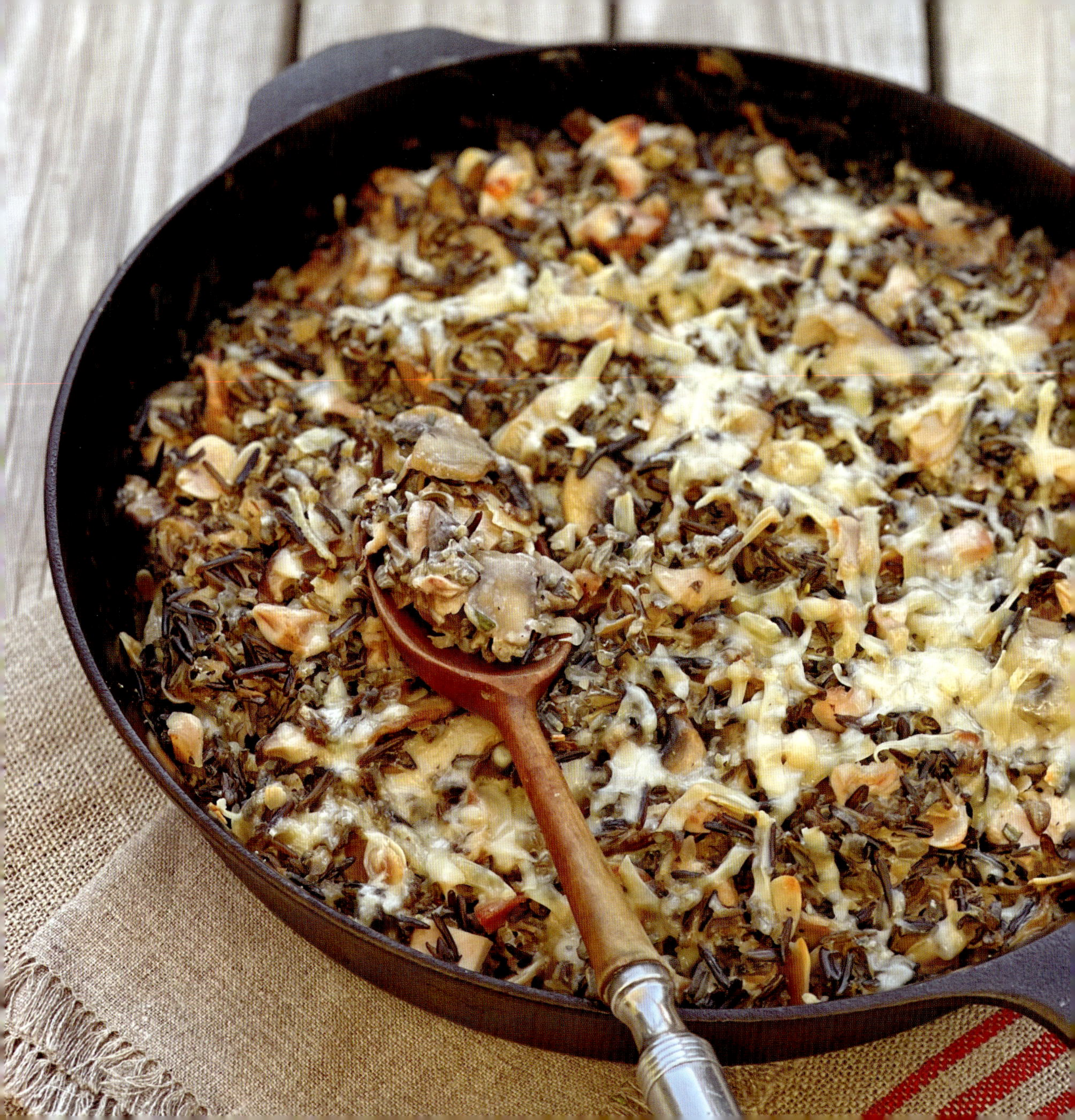

Chicken, Mushroom, and Wild Rice Casserole

This is the ultimate comfort food, combining tender chicken, sliced mushrooms, and a savory
sauce all cooked and baked in a single cast-iron skillet. With the nutty flavor of wild rice and a golden
Parmesan topping, it's a hearty, satisfying dish perfect for family dinners or special occasions.
Best of all, it transitions seamlessly from stovetop to oven, making cleanup a breeze.
Serve it straight from the skillet for a rustic, crowd-pleasing meal that's as easy as it is delicious.

makes 6 to 8 servings

INGREDIENTS

1 cup uncooked wild rice, rinsed

2½ cups chicken broth

1 tablespoon extra-virgin olive oil

1 small onion, finely chopped

1 pound button or cremini
mushrooms, sliced

2 cloves garlic, minced

1 teaspoon fresh (or ¼ teaspoon
dried) thyme leaves

1 teaspoon chopped
fresh rosemary

½ cup sliced toasted almonds

2 cups cooked chicken breast,
shredded or cubed

1 cup sour cream

½ cup half-and-half or milk

¾ teaspoon fine sea salt

½ teaspoon coarsely ground
black pepper

½ cup (2 ounces) freshly grated
Parmesan cheese

Combine rice and broth in a saucepan. Bring to a boil, then reduce heat to low, cover, and simmer for 40 to 45 minutes or until rice is tender and liquid is absorbed. Fluff with a fork and set aside.

Preheat oven to 350°.

Heat olive oil in a large cast-iron or oven-safe skillet over medium heat. Add onion and cook until softened, about 3 to 4 minutes. Add mushrooms and garlic, and sauté until mushrooms release moisture and are golden brown, about 6 to 8 minutes. Stir in thyme and rosemary. Stir in cooked wild rice, almonds, and chicken.

Combine sour cream, half-and-half, salt, and pepper in a bowl; stir into chicken mixture. Spread out evenly. Sprinkle grated Parmesan cheese over top.

Cover with aluminum foil and bake for 20 minutes. Remove foil and continue baking for an additional 15 minutes or until casserole is golden brown and heated through.

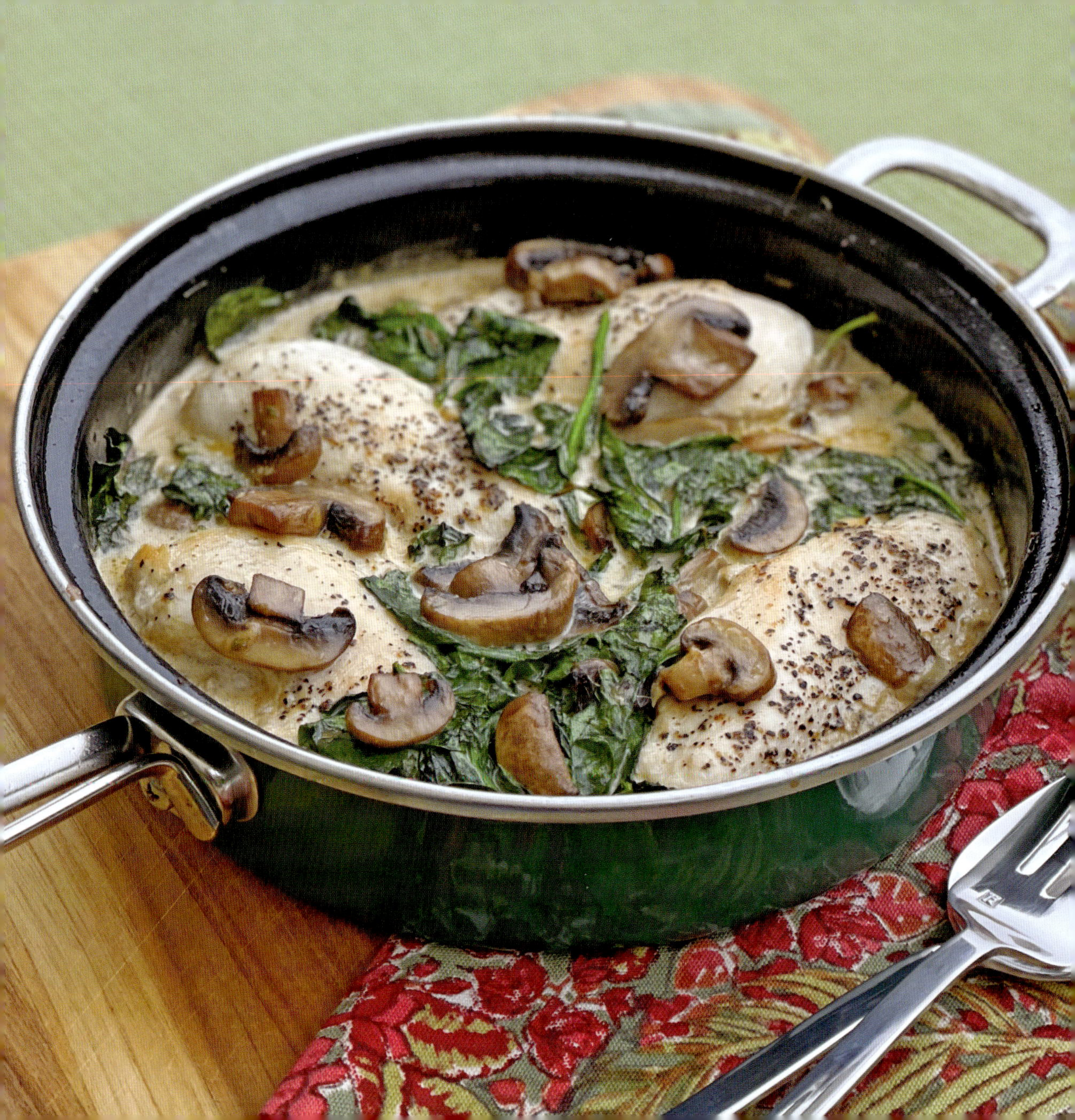

One-Pan Chicken with Mushrooms and Spinach

Using chicken broth lightens the sauce and keeps it from feeling so rich.
Serve this dish in a shallow bowl or a rimmed plate, or serve it
over pasta or mashed potatoes to soak up the flavorful broth.

makes 4 servings

INGREDIENTS

2 tablespoons extra-virgin olive
  oil, divided
4 boneless, skinless
  chicken breasts
1 teaspoon fine sea salt
1 teaspoon coarsely ground
  black pepper
10 ounces (about 2 cups)
  assorted, button, or cremini
  mushrooms, sliced
2 tablespoons vermouth
  or sherry
3 cloves garlic, minced
1 tablespoon fresh (or ½ teaspoon
  dried) thyme leaves
½ cup chicken broth
½ cup heavy cream
¼ cup (1 ounce) freshly grated
  Parmesan cheese
3 cups (2.5 ounces or ½ of a
  5-ounce bag) fresh spinach

Preheat oven to 375°.

Heat 1 tablespoon olive oil in a large oven-safe skillet over medium-high heat. Sprinkle chicken with salt and pepper on both sides. Cook chicken for 3 minutes on each side or until golden brown (chicken doesn't need to be fully cooked). Transfer to a plate and set aside.

Heat remaining 1 tablespoon olive oil over medium-high heat. Add mushrooms and vermouth. Cook for 5 to 7 minutes, stirring occasionally, or until mushrooms begin to brown and most of liquid evaporates. Add garlic and thyme; cook for 1 minute, stirring constantly.

Pour chicken broth into mushroom mixture. Stir in cream and Parmesan cheese. Simmer for 3 to 5 minutes or until mixture starts to thicken. Stir in spinach and cook for 2 to 3 minutes or until wilted. Remove from heat and arrange chicken breasts in sauce, spooning sauce over each.

Bake for 15 to 20 minutes or until chicken reaches an internal temperature of 165° and is fully cooked through.

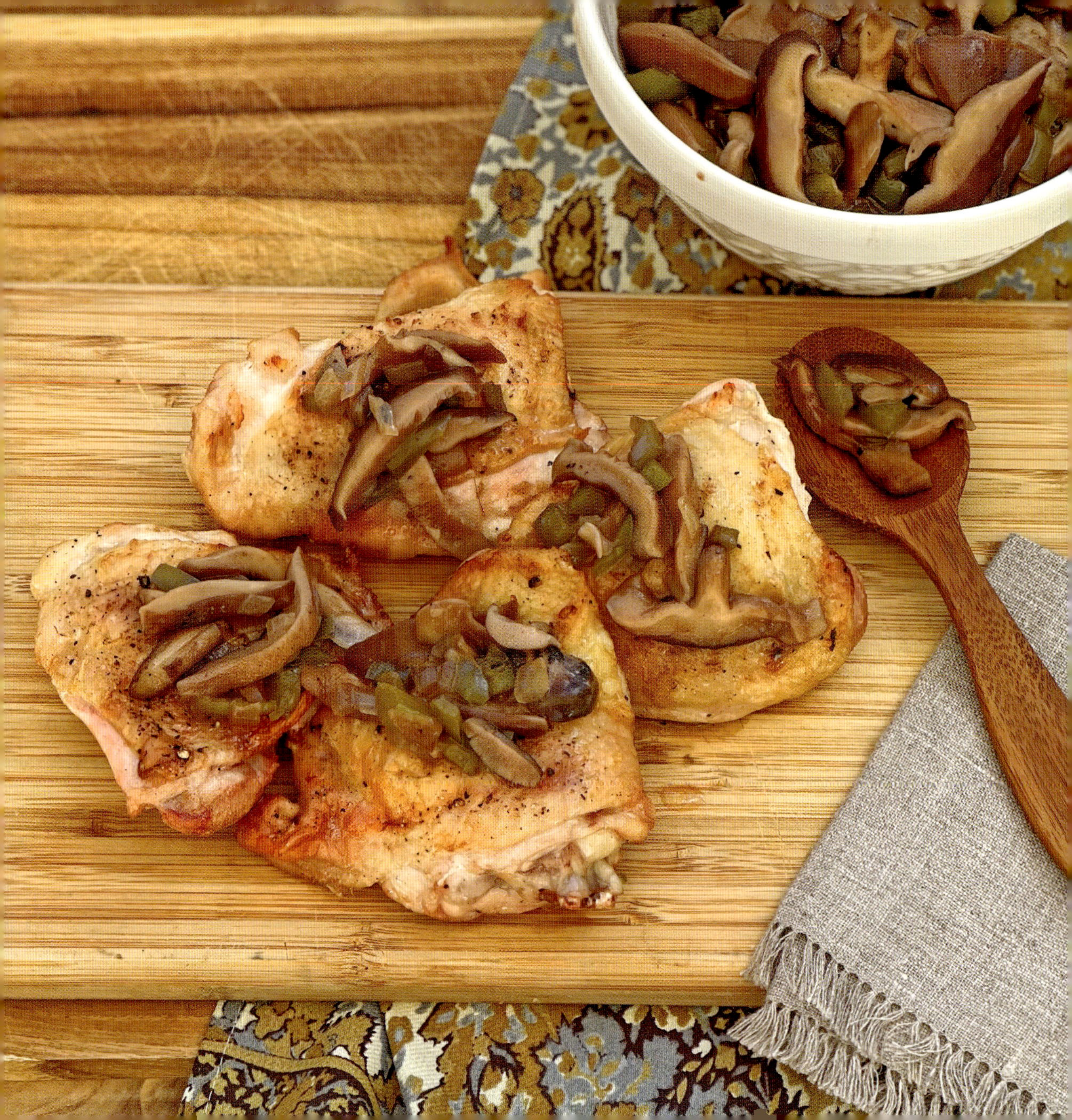

Grilled Meat with Mushroom Berkeley Sauce

There is a type of foraged wild mushroom commonly called Berkeley, and perhaps that's where this strongly flavored sauce gets its name. A mix of mushrooms pairs well here. If using button mushrooms as a substitute, you won't get much of a mushroom flavor because the red wine and Dijon mustard will dominate. Ideal with venison or roast pork, the sauce can also be spooned over milder meats like grilled chicken.

makes 4 to 6 servings

INGREDIENTS

2 tablespoons butter
1 green bell pepper, coarsely chopped
¼ large onion, finely chopped
15 to 16 ounces assorted mushrooms (shiitake, oyster, and/or cremini)
½ cup red wine
¼ cup firmly packed light brown sugar
1½ tablespoons Worcestershire sauce
1½ tablespoons Dijon mustard
¼ teaspoon coarsely ground black pepper
⅛ teaspoon fine sea salt
Grilled chicken, steak, or wild game

Melt butter in a Dutch oven or saucepan over medium heat. Add bell pepper and onion. Cook, stirring frequently, for 5 minutes or until tender. Add mushrooms. Cook, stirring frequently, for 5 to 7 minutes or until mushrooms are tender and liquid evaporates.

Combine wine, brown sugar, Worcestershire, mustard, pepper, and salt in a small bowl, stirring until smooth.

Stir wine mixture into mushroom mixture. Bring mixture to a boil, reduce heat, and simmer for 3 to 5 minutes or until sauce reduces and thickens. Serve over grilled meat.

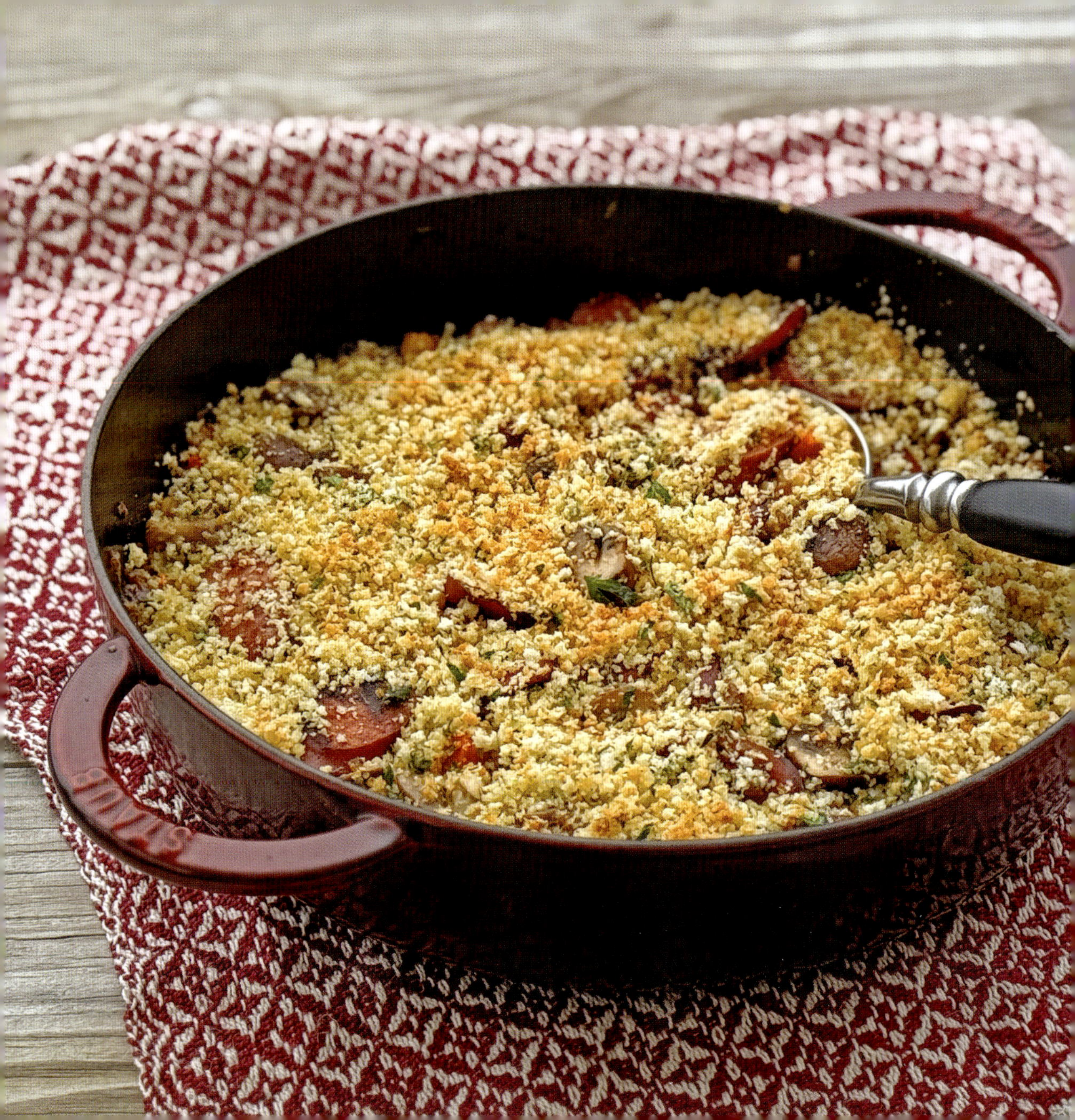

Quick Mushroom-and-Sausage Cassoulet

This comforting twist on the classic French dish is designed for busy weeknights.

makes 6 servings

INGREDIENTS

4 tablespoons extra-virgin olive oil, divided

1¼ pounds assorted mushrooms (shiitake, oyster, and/or cremini), sliced or quartered

12 ounces smoked kielbasa or meatless sausage, sliced

1 onion, chopped

2 carrots, diced

2 garlic cloves, finely chopped

2 teaspoons chopped fresh rosemary

2 teaspoons fresh thyme leaves

1 tablespoon tomato paste

¼ teaspoon smoked paprika

2 (15-ounce) cans cannellini beans, rinsed and drained

1 cup mushroom or chicken broth

½ teaspoon fine sea salt

½ teaspoon coarsely ground black pepper

Panko Topping (recipe at right)

Preheat oven to 400°.

Heat 2 tablespoons oil in a large cassoulet over medium-high heat. Add mushrooms and cook, stirring frequently, for 5 minutes or until browned. Transfer to a plate. Heat 1 tablespoon oil in same pan over medium-high heat. Add sausage and cook, stirring occasionally, for 3 minutes or until browned. Transfer to plate. Add remaining 1 tablespoon oil to pan over medium-high heat. Add onion and carrots. Cook, stirring frequently, for 4 minutes. Stir in garlic, rosemary, and thyme; cook for 1 minute, stirring constantly. Add tomato paste and paprika; cook, stirring constantly, for 1 minute.

Stir in beans, broth, mushrooms, sausage, ½ teaspoon salt, and pepper. Bring mixture to a simmer. Remove from heat and sprinkle evenly with Panko Topping.

Bake, uncovered, for 15 minutes or until golden brown and bubbly.

Panko Topping: Combine **1 cup seasoned panko, 2 tablespoons melted butter, 3 tablespoons finely grated Parmesan cheese, 1 tablespoon chopped fresh parsley,** and **⅛ teaspoon fine sea salt** in a bowl. Makes 1 cup.

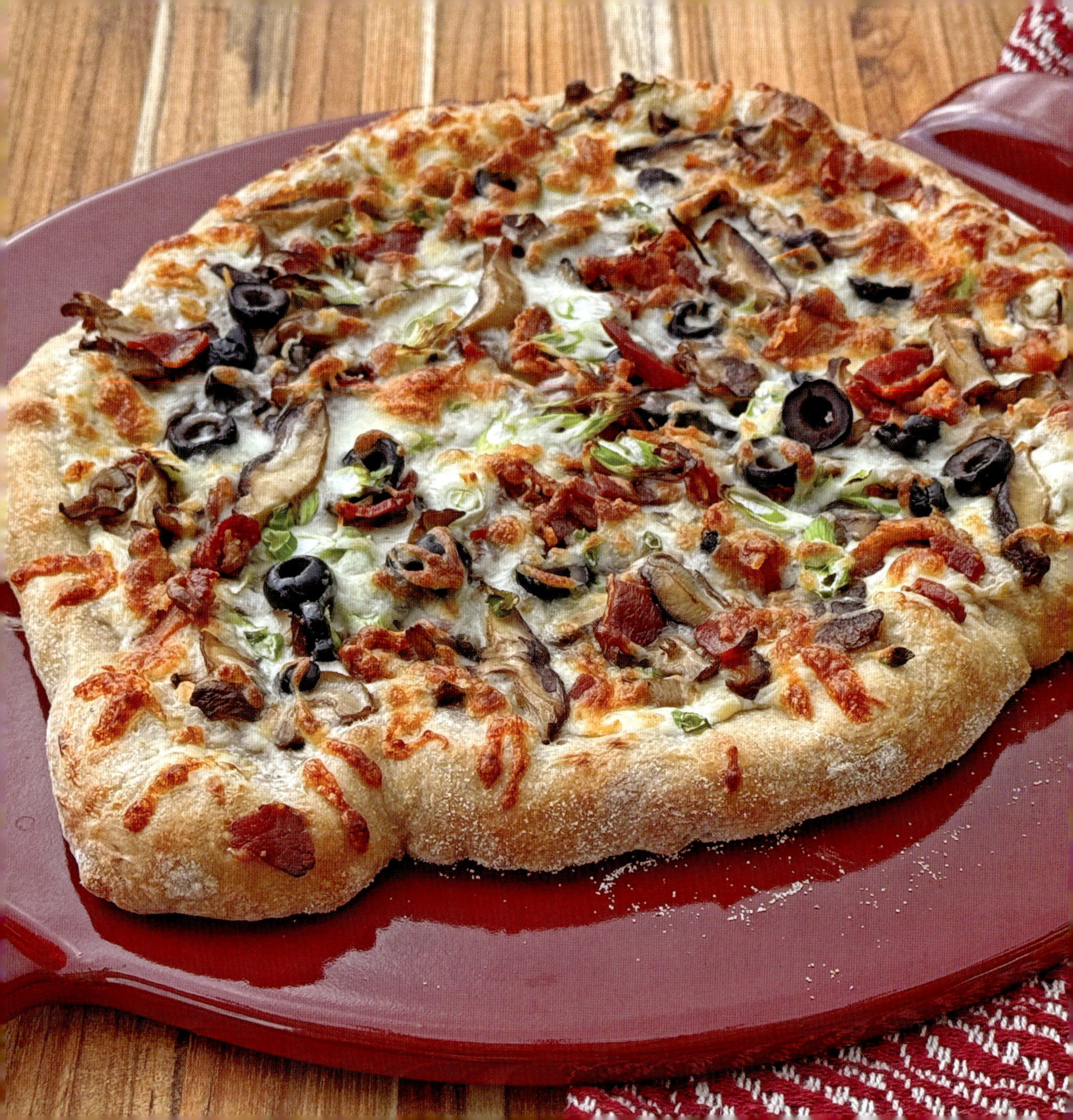

Mushroom-and-Bacon White Sauce Pizza

Try this gourmet twist on a classic favorite, featuring a rich white sauce.

makes 2 to 4 servings

INGREDIENTS

1 tablespoon extra-virgin olive oil

1 pound assorted mushrooms (shiitake, oyster, and/or cremini), sliced or cut into bite-size pieces

½ teaspoon fine sea salt

1 (16-ounce) ball of pizza dough

Semolina, cornmeal, or all-purpose flour

½ cup Garlic-Parmesan White Sauce (recipe at right) or ½ cup store-bought Alfredo sauce

4 slices cooked bacon, chopped

⅓ cup sliced black olives

1 cup (4 ounces) shredded mozzarella cheese

¼ cup (1 ounce) freshly shredded or grated Parmesan cheese

Heat oil in a large skillet over medium-high heat. Add mushrooms and ½ teaspoon salt. Cook, stirring frequently, for 5 to 7 minutes or until mushrooms are tender and liquid evaporates. Set aside.

Preheat oven to 450°.

Roll dough to ¼-inch thickness on a lightly floured surface. Spread Garlic-Parmesan White Sauce to edges of dough. Top with reserved mushrooms, bacon, olives, and cheeses.

Transfer pizza to a greased (with olive oil) baking sheet dusted with semolina or cornmeal. Bake for 10 to 12 minutes or until hot and bubbly.

Garlic-Parmesan White Sauce: Melt **2 tablespoons butter** in a saucepan over medium heat. Add **2 minced garlic cloves** and cook, stirring frequently, for 2 minutes or until fragrant but not browned. Stir in **1 tablespoon all-purpose flour.** Cook for 1 to 2 minutes, stirring constantly, until mixture is pale gold. Whisk in **1 cup half-and-half.** Cook, whisking constantly, for 3 minutes or until sauce begins to thicken. Stir in **¼ cup (1 ounce) freshly shredded Parmesan cheese, ¼ teaspoon salt**, and **¼ teaspoon coarsely ground black pepper.** Cook, stirring frequently, until smooth. Makes about 1 cup (enough for 2 pizzas).

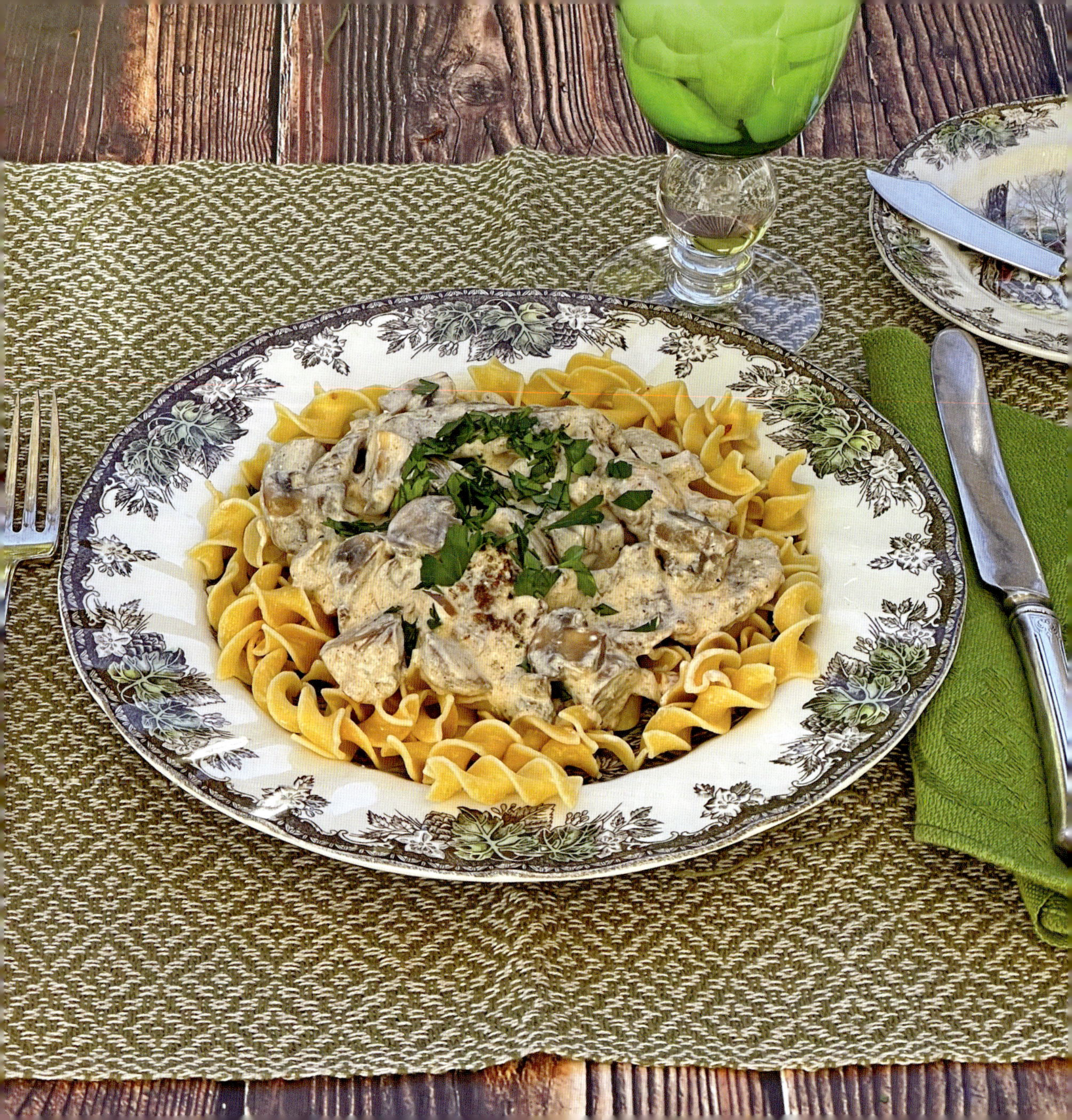

Beef-and-Mushroom Stroganoff

This classic comfort food is wonderfully versatile—use any cut of beef on sale or a combination of cuts. Egg noodles pair perfectly with the rich mushroom gravy, whether you prefer wide or narrow varieties.

INGREDIENTS

- 3 tablespoons all-purpose flour
- 1 teaspoon paprika
- ⅛ teaspoon cayenne pepper
- 1½ teaspoons fine sea salt, divided
- ½ teaspoon coarsely ground black pepper, divided
- 1 pound beef sirloin, boneless rib eye, or tenderloin
- 2 tablespoons extra-virgin olive or vegetable oil, divided
- 4 tablespoons salted or unsalted butter, divided
- 1 pound button or cremini mushrooms, quartered
- ½ small white or yellow onion, finely chopped
- ¼ cup dry white wine
- ¾ cup beef broth
- 1 cup sour cream
- 1 teaspoon Worcestershire sauce
- 1 (12-ounce) package egg noodles
- 2 tablespoons chopped fresh parsley

Combine flour, paprika, cayenne pepper, ½ teaspoon salt, and ¼ teaspoon black pepper in a large shallow dish.

Slice beef against the grain into ½-inch strips. Pound lightly to ¼-inch thickness. Dredge meat in flour mixture, shaking off excess.

Heat 1 tablespoon oil in a large skillet over medium-high heat. Add half of the beef and cook for 1 to 2 minutes or until browned on all sides. Transfer to a plate and repeat with remaining 1 tablespoon oil and remaining beef. Transfer meat to a plate; cover with aluminum foil to keep warm.

Melt 2 tablespoons butter in same skillet (no need to wipe clean) over medium-high heat. Add mushrooms, onion, remaining 1 teaspoon salt, and remaining ¼ teaspoon pepper. Cook, stirring frequently, for 10 to 12 minutes or until golden brown and most of the liquid has evaporated. Add wine, stirring well. Cook until liquid is mostly evaporated. Stir in broth, sour cream, Worcestershire, reserved beef, and any juices. Keep warm over low heat; do not boil.

Meanwhile, cook noodles in boiling water according to package directions. Drain and transfer to a bowl. Add remaining 2 tablespoons butter; toss until butter melts and coats noodles.

Serve beef mixture over noodles, and sprinkle with parsley.

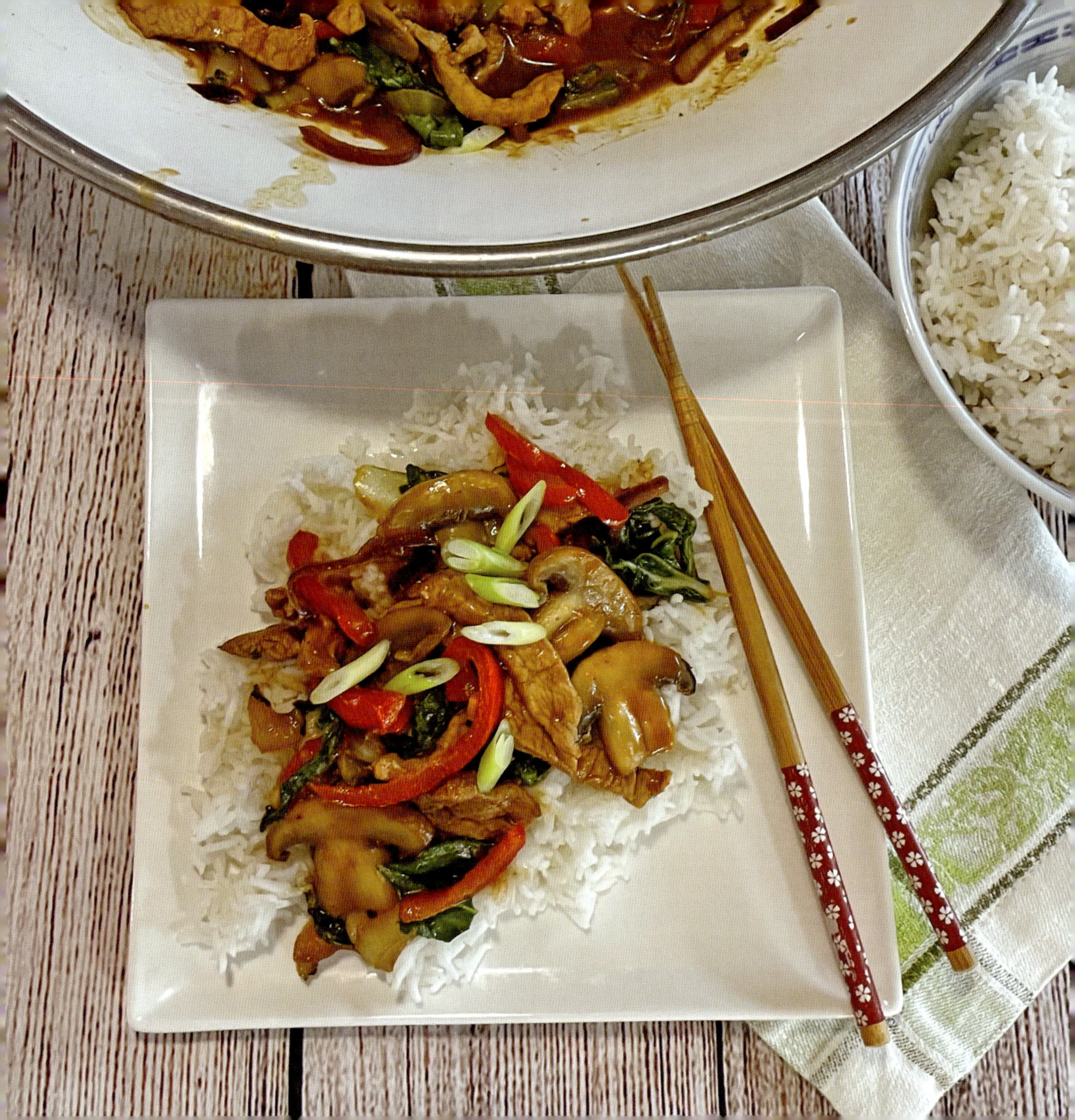

Garlic Pork with Mushrooms

This stir-fry with mushrooms and bok choy is a flavorful meal that comes together in minutes.
Tender slices of pork are cooked with tasty mushrooms, crisp bok choy, and a spicy
sauce made with gochujang or chili garlic paste. The combination of heat, umami,
and fresh greens creates a well-balanced dish that's perfect served over a bed of hot rice.

makes 4 servings

INGREDIENTS

½ cup chicken or vegetable broth
⅓ cup hoisin sauce
3 tablespoons low-sodium
  soy sauce
1 tablespoon rice vinegar
1 tablespoon cornstarch
½ teaspoon gochujang,
  chili-garlic paste, or hot sauce
1¼ pounds pork loin or
  tenderloin, cut into strips
2 small heads or 1 large head
  bok choy
2 tablespoons vegetable oil,
  divided
8 ounces cremini or button
  mushrooms, sliced
1 red bell pepper, thinly sliced
1 small red onion,
  halved and sliced
5 large garlic cloves, sliced
1 tablespoon minced
  fresh ginger
2 green onions, sliced
Hot cooked rice

Combine broth, hoisin, soy sauce, rice vinegar, cornstarch, and gochujang paste in a small bowl. Transfer ¼ cup sauce mixture to a large bowl. Add pork and marinate for 30 minutes.

Trim root end of bok choy. Slice white stems. Tear leaves into pieces and set aside.

Heat 1 tablespoon oil in a wok or large deep skillet over medium-high heat. Add pork; stir-fry for 3 minutes or until meat is browned. Transfer to a plate. Wipe wok clean.

Heat remaining 1 tablespoon oil in same wok over medium-high heat. Add reserved bok choy stems, mushrooms, bell pepper, and red onion. Stir-fry for 5 minutes or until vegetables are softened. Add garlic and ginger; stir-fry for 30 seconds or until fragrant.

Return cooked pork to wok. Stir in reserved marinade mixture and bok choy leaves. Bring to a boil, reduce heat, and simmer for 1 to 2 minutes or until leaves wilt and mixture thickens. Sprinkle with green onions and serve over hot cooked rice.

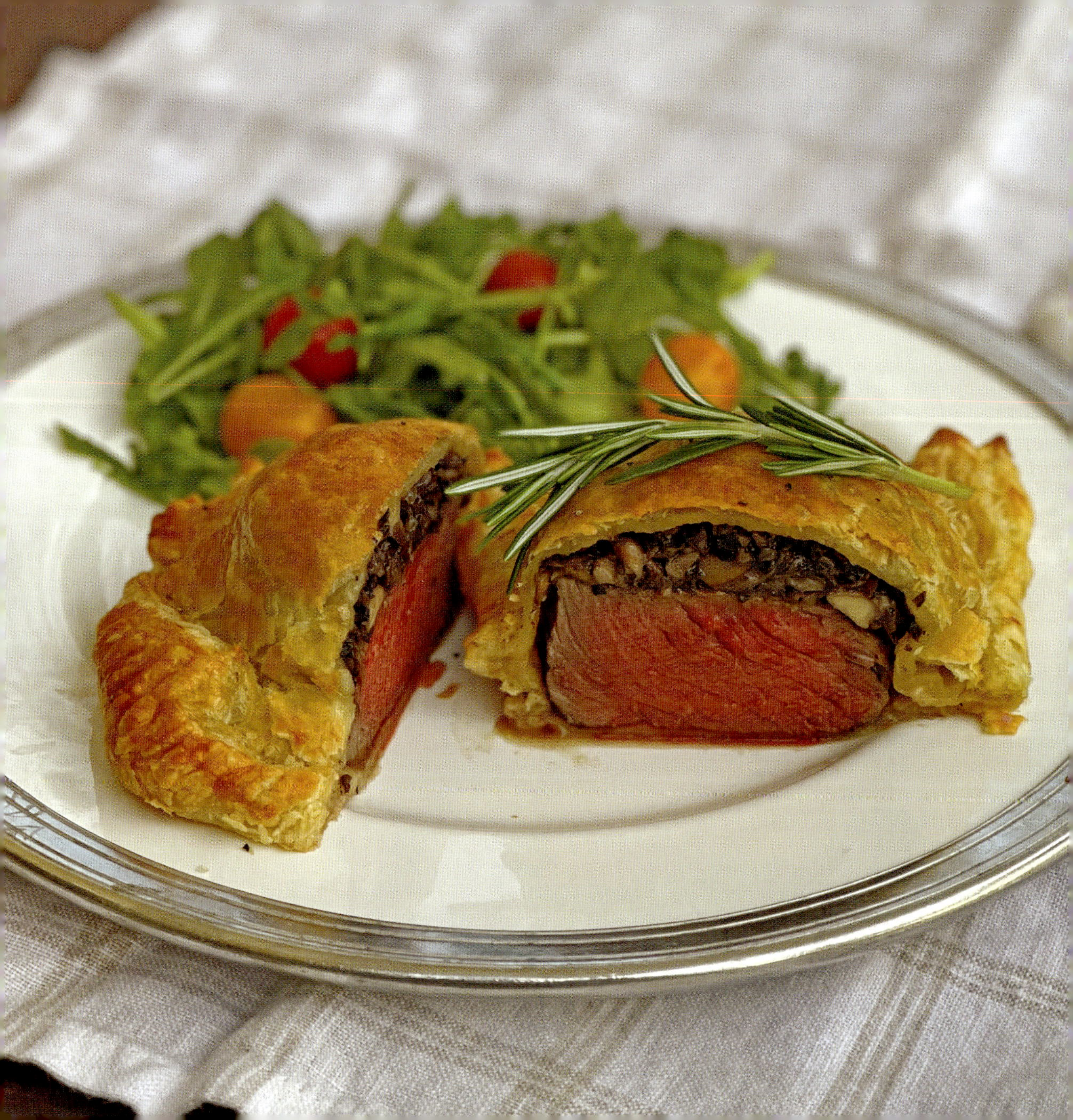

Individual Beef Wellingtons

Feel free to substitute shiitake, maitake, or oyster mushrooms.
Instead of salt, stir in a dash of tamari or soy sauce.

makes 4 servings

INGREDIENTS

4 (6- to 8-ounce)
   beef tenderloin steaks
1 teaspoon seasoned salt blend
1 tablespoon avocado or
   extra-virgin olive oil
2 tablespoons salted or
   unsalted butter
1 tablespoon extra-virgin olive oil
1 shallot, finely chopped
2 garlic cloves, minced
8 ounces cremini or button
   mushrooms, finely chopped
2 teaspoons fresh (or ½ teaspoon
   dried) thyme
2 tablespoons red wine or sherry
½ teaspoon fine sea salt
¼ teaspoon coarsely ground
   black pepper
2 sheets refrigerated or frozen-
   and-thawed puff pastry
1 large egg, lightly beaten
1 tablespoon water

GARNISH

fresh rosemary sprigs

Preheat oven to 400°.

Preheat a large cast-iron skillet over medium-high heat. Sprinkle steaks evenly with seasoned salt. Drizzle avocado oil in skillet and add steaks. Sear on each side for about 2 minutes, then cook on the sides for about 30 seconds to develop a brown crust. Remove from skillet and set aside.

Add butter and olive oil to same skillet (no need to wipe clean) over medium heat. Add shallot and garlic. Cook, stirring frequently, for about 2 minutes. Add mushrooms and thyme and cook, stirring frequently, for 5 to 7 minutes or until mushrooms release moisture and begin to brown. Add wine and cook for 2 minutes or until evaporated. Stir in salt and pepper. Remove from heat and set aside.

Roll out puff pastry sheets and cut each into 4 equal squares (8 total). Place a steak in center of each of 4 squares. Top steaks evenly with mushroom mixture. Top with remaining 4 squares. Combine egg with 1 tablespoon water. Brush top and edges with egg mixture and fold seams, pressing with a fork to seal.

Place Wellingtons on a baking sheet lined with parchment paper. Bake for 20 to 25 minutes or until golden brown and medium rare. Insert a meat thermometer into side and cook to desired degree of doneness. Garnish, if desired.

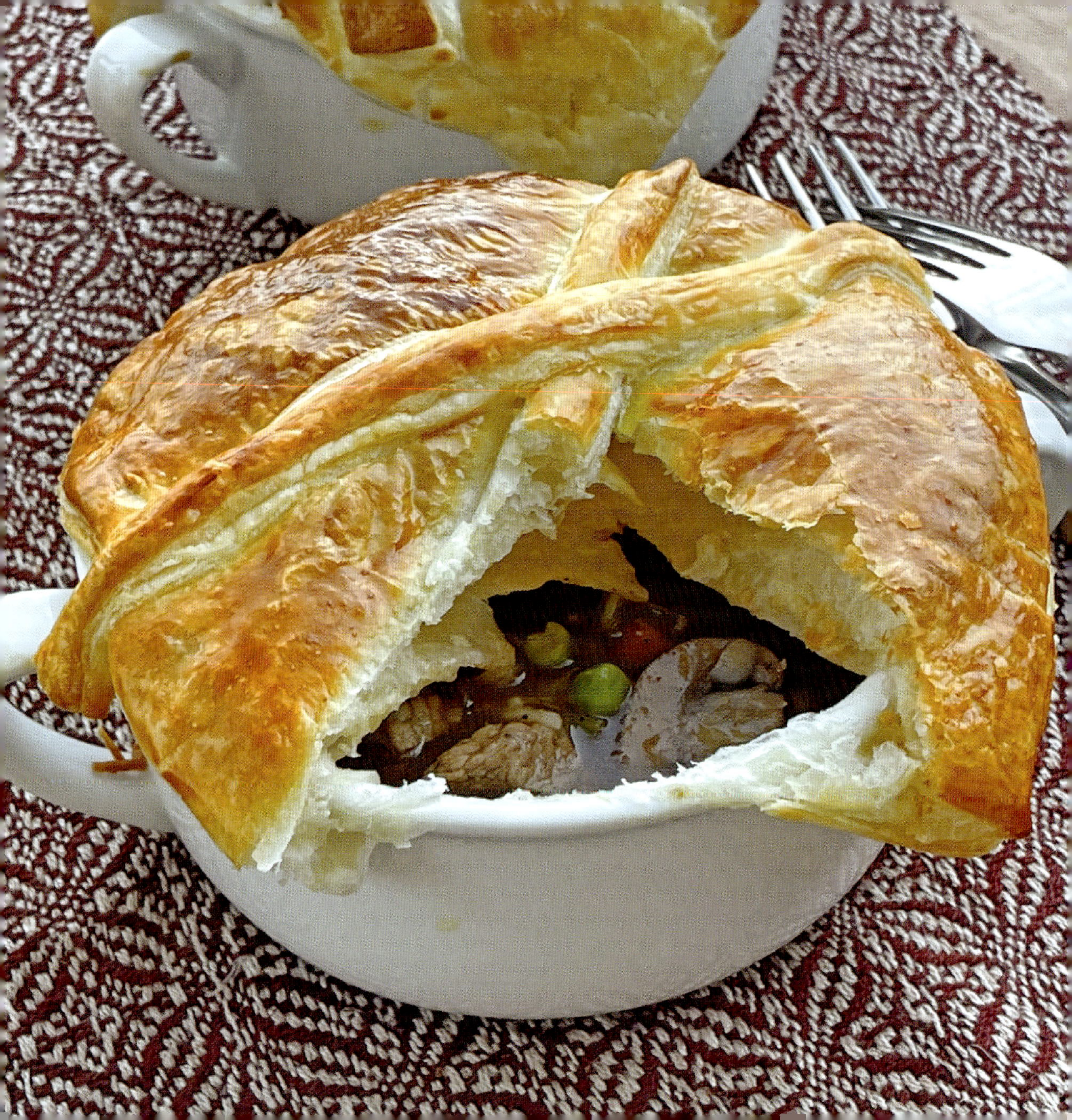

Beef-and-Mushroom Pot Pies

These pot pies are a comforting classic, made even more convenient with individual servings. Tucked beneath golden, flaky pastry, these tasty delights are perfect for cozy dinners or entertaining.

INGREDIENTS

2 tablespoons extra-virgin olive oil, divided
1½ pounds beef stew meat, cut into bite-size pieces
1 teaspoon fine sea salt, divided
¾ teaspoon coarsely ground black pepper, divided
½ small onion, chopped
2 carrots, peeled and diced
2 celery ribs, chopped
1 (8-ounce) package button, cremini or other mushrooms, sliced
2 garlic cloves, minced
¼ cup all-purpose flour
½ cup red wine
1½ cups beef stock or broth
1 teaspoon Worcestershire sauce
1 teaspoon fresh thyme
1 teaspoon fresh rosemary
1 cup frozen peas
1 sheet refrigerated or frozen-and-thawed puff pastry
1 egg, beaten

Preheat oven to 400°.

Heat 1 tablespoon olive oil in a large deep skillet or Dutch oven over medium-high heat. Sprinkle beef with ½ teaspoon salt and ¼ teaspoon pepper. Cook for 3 to 4 minutes or until browned on all sides. Transfer to a plate and set aside.

Heat remaining 1 tablespoon olive oil in skillet (no need to wipe clean). Add onion, carrots, celery, and mushrooms. Cook, stirring frequently, for 5 to 7 minutes or until vegetables are tender. Add garlic and cook for 1 minute.

Sprinkle flour over vegetables and stir to combine. Cook for 2 to 3 minutes. Gradually stir in red wine and cook for 1 minute or until thickened. Stir in broth, Worcestershire, thyme, rosemary, remaining ½ teaspoon salt, and remaining ¼ teaspoon pepper. Return beef to skillet. Bring mixture to a boil, reduce heat, and simmer for 15 minutes or until mixture thickens and beef is tender. Stir in peas. Transfer beef mixture to 4 (2-cup) individual ramekins or oven-safe soup bowls.

Roll out puff pastry and cut into 4 squares. Place 1 pastry square over top of each ramekin, crimping edges to seal. If desired, use any scraps to decorate the top. Brush pastry with beaten egg. Place pot pies on a rimmed baking sheet. Bake for 20 to 25 minutes or until crust is golden brown and crisp.

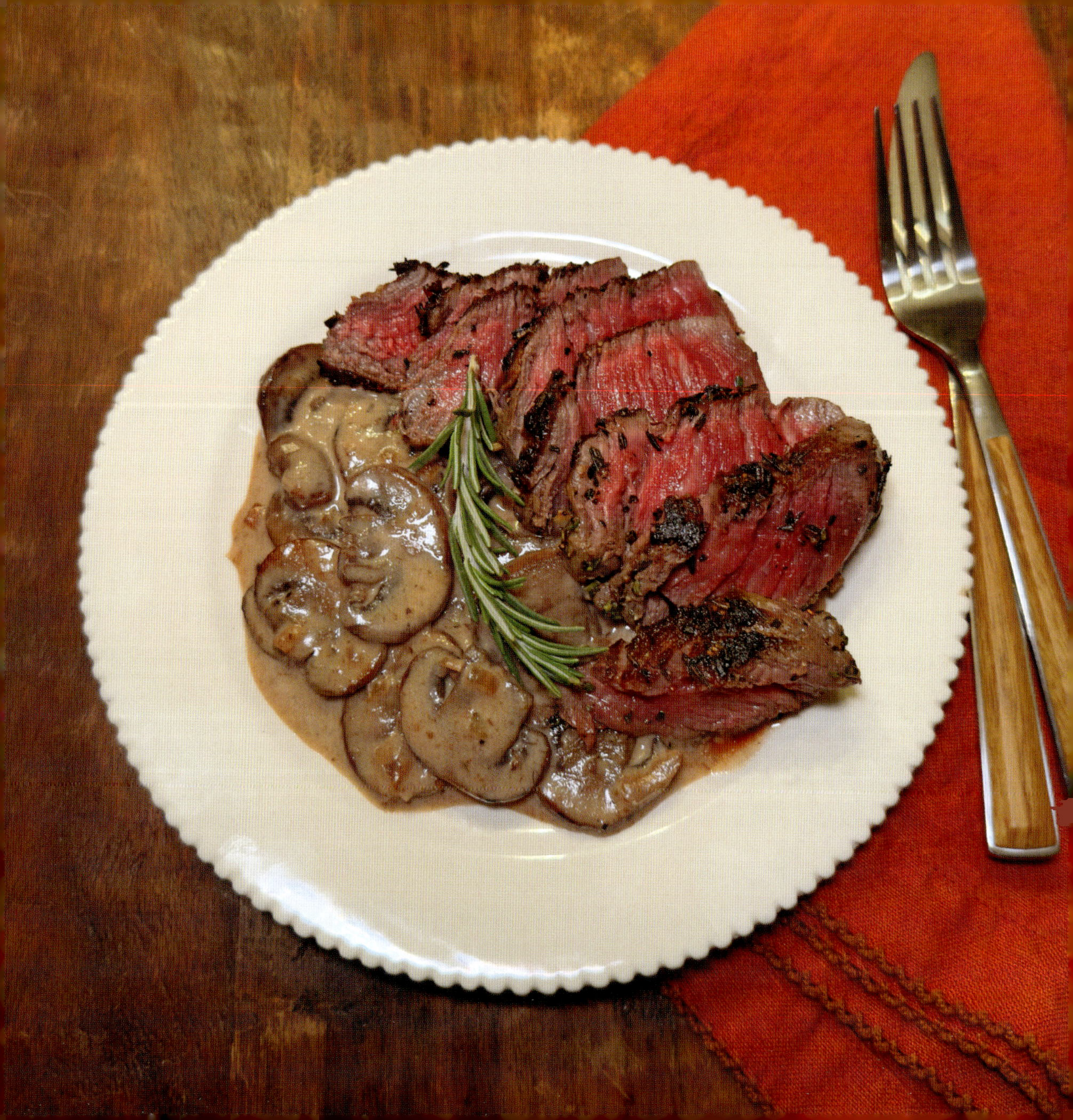

Grilled Steaks with Pinot-Mushroom Sauce

This elegant-yet-approachable dish is perfect for a special occasion or a cozy dinner at home. The sauce, featuring a medley of sautéed mushrooms and the subtle sweetness of Pinot Noir, complements the beef's natural flavor without overpowering it. Serve this with roasted vegetables or creamy mashed potatoes for a restaurant-quality meal that's surprisingly simple to prepare.

makes 2 cups (4 servings)

INGREDIENTS

- 2 tablespoons unsalted butter
- 1 tablespoon extra-virgin olive oil
- 1 pound assorted mushrooms (cremini, button, or shiitake), sliced
- ½ small onion, finely chopped
- 2 cloves garlic, minced
- ½ cup Pinot Noir or other red wine
- 1 cup beef stock or broth
- ½ cup heavy cream
- ½ teaspoon fine sea salt
- ¼ teaspoon coarsely ground black pepper
- 4 Grilled Steaks (recipe at right)

Heat butter and 1 tablespoon oil in a large skillet over medium heat. Add mushrooms, onion, and 2 cloves minced garlic. Cook, stirring frequently, for 6 to 8 minutes or until mushrooms release moisture and are golden brown.

Pour in wine. Cook, stirring occasionally, for 4 minutes or until wine is almost evaporated. Stir in broth. Bring wine mixture to a simmer and cook for 5 minutes or until slightly thickened. Stir in cream and simmer for 2 to 3 minutes. Stir in ½ teaspoon salt and ¼ teaspoon pepper. Serve with Grilled Steaks.

Grilled Steaks: Combine **2 tablespoons extra-virgin olive oil, 2 minced garlic cloves, 2 tablespoons chopped fresh rosemary, ½ teaspoon fine sea salt,** and **½ teaspoon coarsely ground black pepper** in a small bowl. Rub mixture evenly over all sides of 4 (6- to 8-ounce) beef tenderloin, ribeye, or sirloin steaks. Let stand at room temperature for 30 minutes. Preheat grill to medium-high heat. Grill for 4 to 5 minutes on each side for medium rare or until desired degree of doneness. Cover with aluminum foil and let rest for 10 minutes. Makes 4 servings.

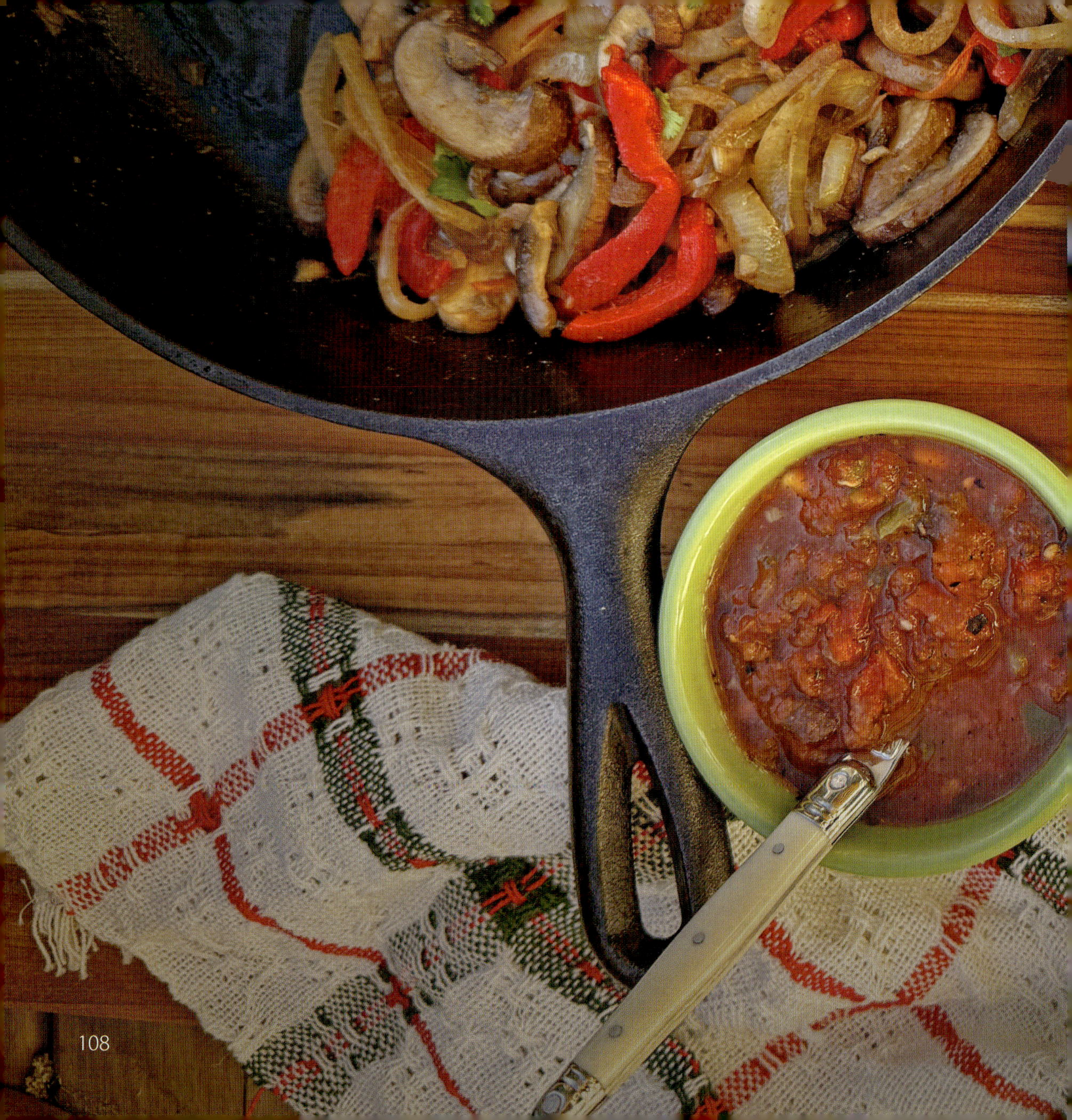

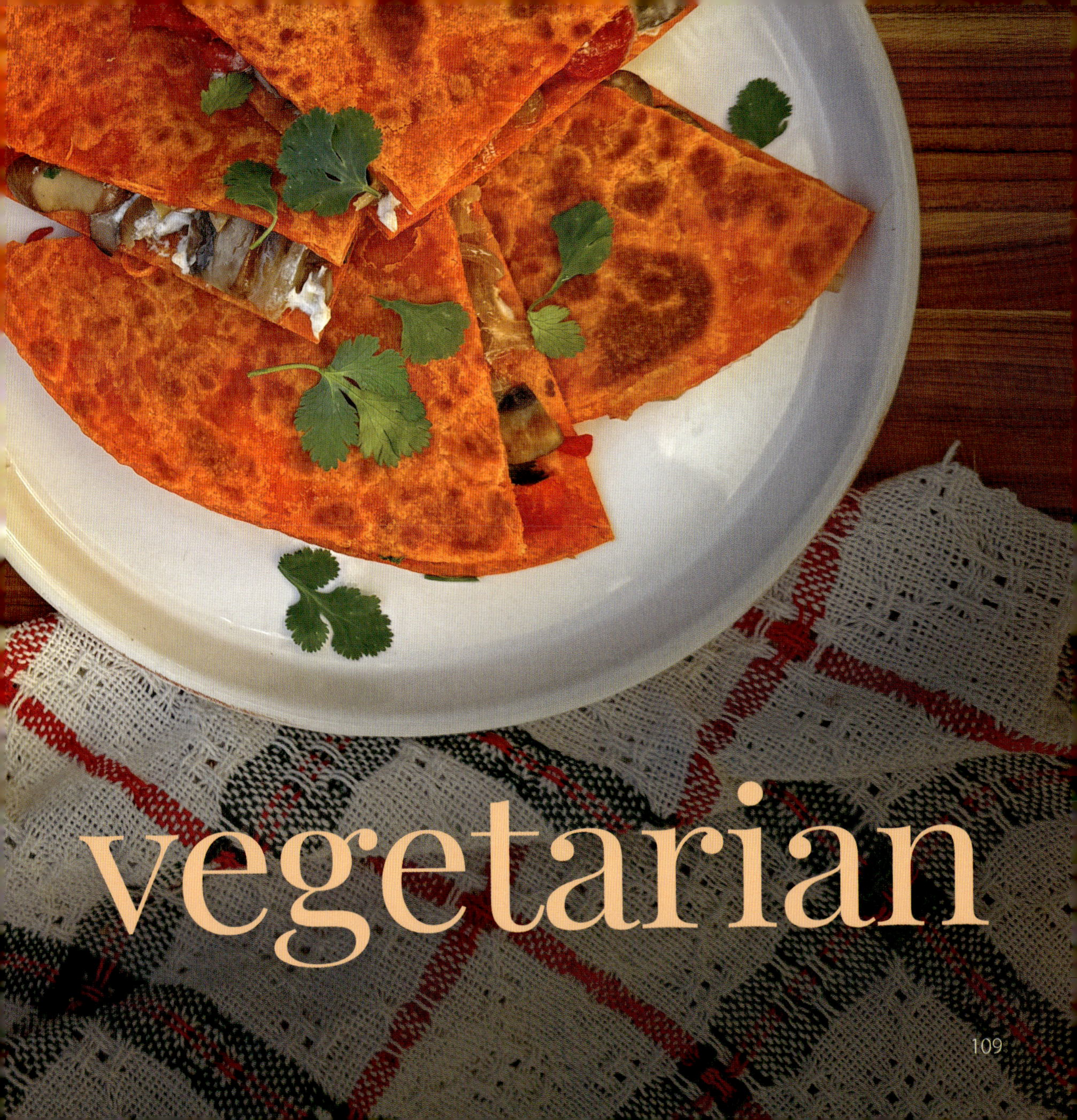

vegetarian

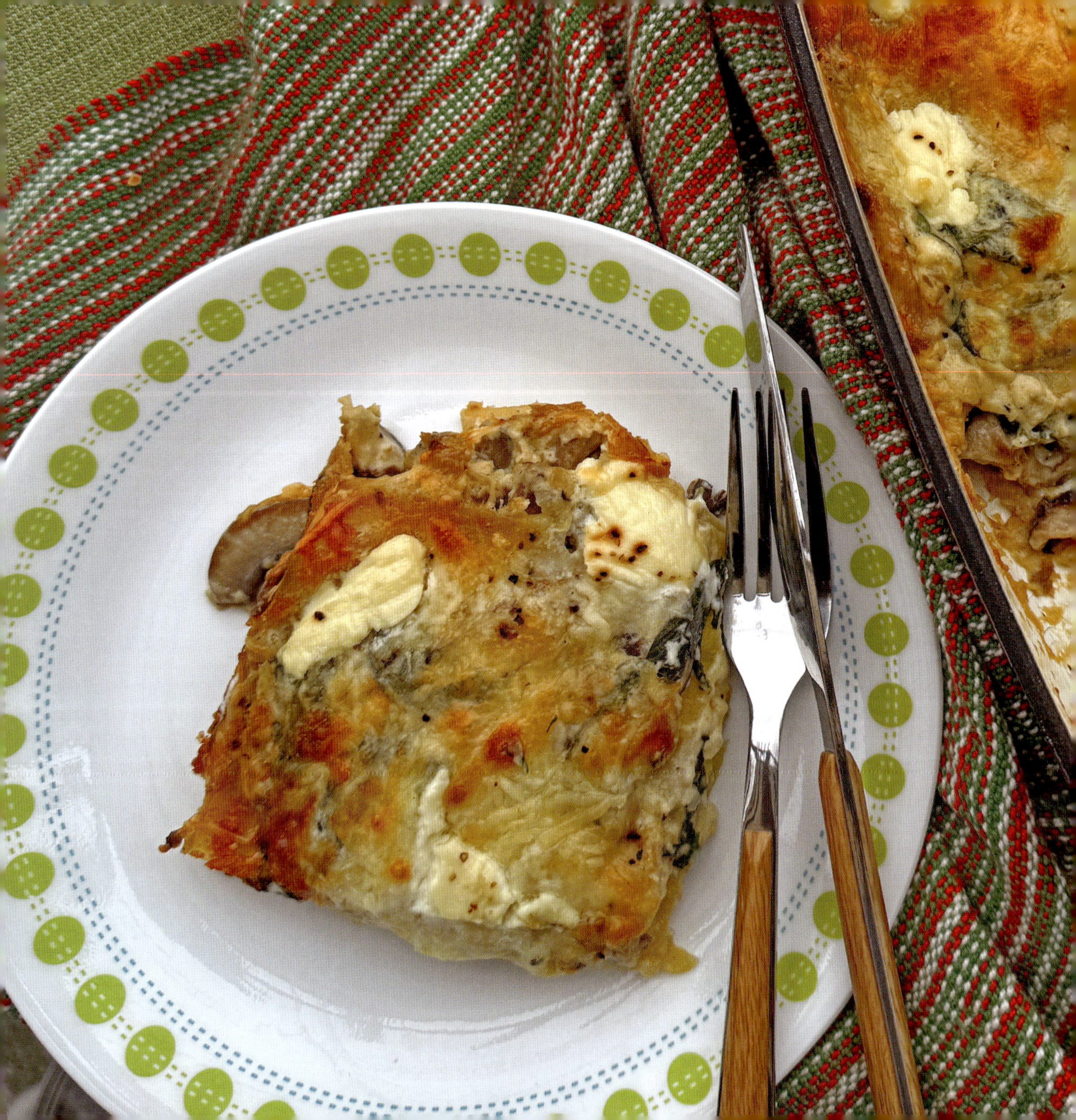

Mushroom-and-Spinach Lasagna

Whether you're feeding a crowd or meal-prepping for the week, this lasagna is sure to impress.

makes 8 servings

INGREDIENTS

- 9 uncooked or 12 oven-ready lasagna noodles
- 4 tablespoons unsalted or salted butter
- 1 pound shiitake and oyster mushrooms
- 1 onion, chopped
- 2 large garlic cloves, finely chopped
- ½ teaspoon dried Italian seasoning
- ½ teaspoon fine sea salt
- ½ teaspoon coarsely ground black pepper
- ¼ cup all-purpose flour
- 3 tablespoons sherry or white wine
- 2½ cups half-and-half
- ¼ teaspoon ground nutmeg
- 5 ounces baby spinach
- 1 cup (4 ounces) shredded mozzarella cheese, divided
- ½ cup (2 ounces) freshly shredded Parmesan cheese, divided
- 1 cup ricotta cheese

Preheat oven to 375°. Lightly grease (with butter) a 13x9-inch baking dish.

Cook lasagna noodles in boiling salted water according to package directions. Drain; set aside.

Melt butter in a large skillet over medium-high heat. Add mushrooms, onion, garlic, Italian seasoning, salt, and pepper. Cook, stirring frequently, for 5 to 8 minutes or until mushrooms are tender and most of the liquid evaporates.

Add flour and cook, stirring constantly, for 1 minute. Stir in sherry and cook, stirring constantly, for 1 minute or until sherry evaporates. Slowly stir in half-and-half and nutmeg. Cook over medium heat for 5 to 7 minutes or until mushroom mixture thickens. Add spinach, stirring until spinach wilts.

Spread about 2 cups mushroom sauce in bottom of prepared dish. Top with one-third lasagna noodles. Top with 1 cup mushroom sauce, one-third mozzarella, and one-third Parmesan cheese. Dollop one-third ricotta around top of mixture. Repeat layers twice, starting with noodles.

Cover with aluminum foil and bake for 30 minutes. Uncover and bake for 20 to 25 minutes or until golden brown and bubbly.

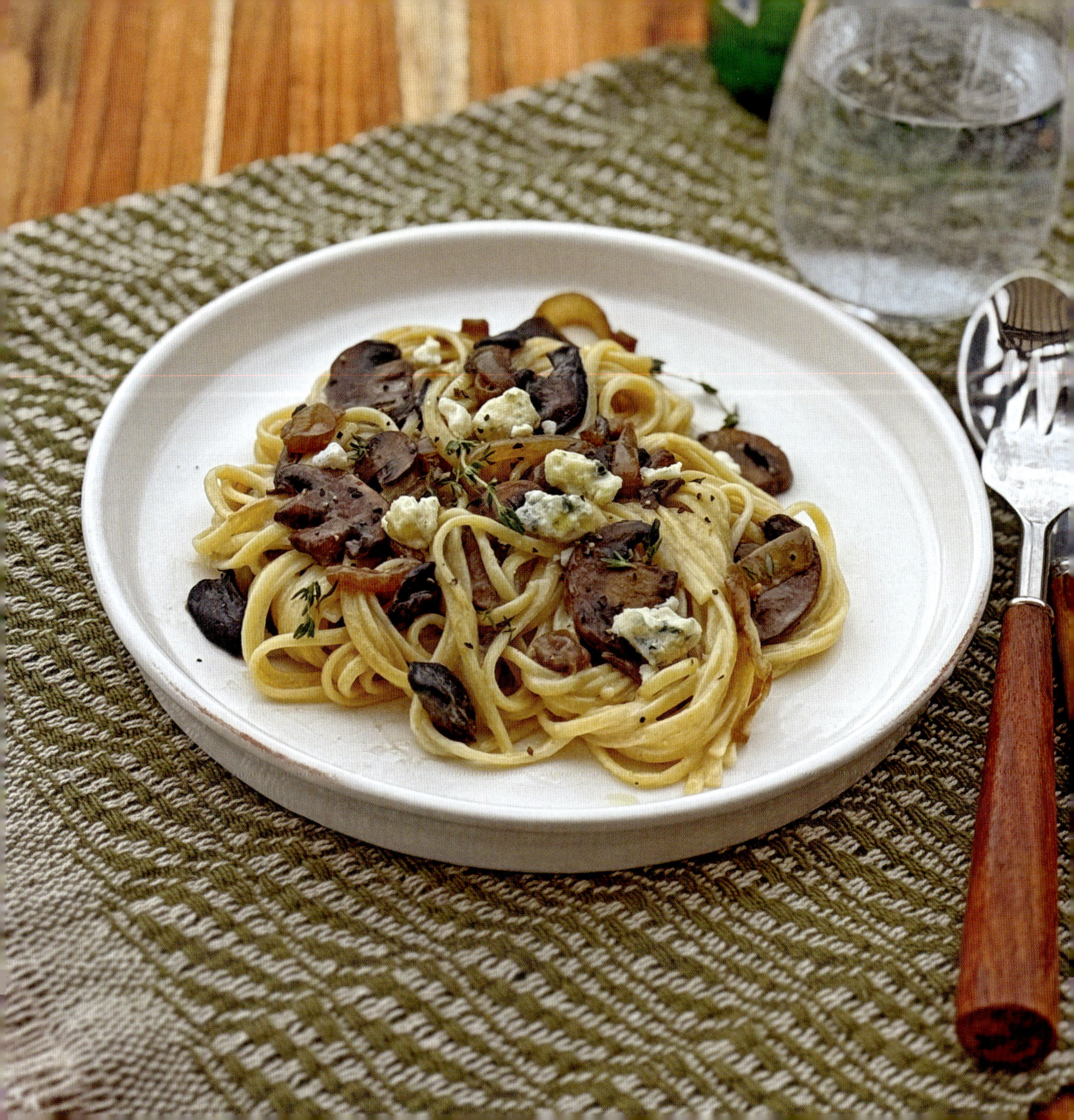

Caramelized Onion-and-Mushroom Pasta

Caramelized onions take a while to reach their beautiful golden-brown color, but the wait is worth it! This recipe requires patience but is otherwise very simple. I was playing around with the onion-and-mushroom mixture when I realized it would be delicious as a tart filling (see page 45) or doubled as a pasta topper. Hot cooked pasta is simply dressed in mascarpone cheese, which melts and coats the noodles with a creamy, luscious sauce that enhances the umami essence of the onions and mushrooms.

INGREDIENTS

2 tablespoons extra-virgin olive oil
2 large sweet onions, halved and sliced
1 teaspoon fine sea salt
3 tablespoons balsamic vinegar
1 pound cremini or other mushroom, sliced
12 ounces linguini or other pasta
1 (8-ounce) container mascarpone cheese
⅓ cup crumbled blue, feta, or goat cheese

Heat olive oil in an extra-large skillet over medium heat. Add onions and salt, stirring until well blended. Cook, stirring occasionally, for 20 minutes or until onions are a light golden brown.

Stir in balsamic vinegar and mushrooms. Cook, stirring occasionally, for 15 minutes or until mushrooms are tender and onions are a rich dark brown.

Cook pasta according to package directions. Drain and transfer to a large bowl. Add mascarpone, stirring until well coated. Stir in mushroom mixture. Top servings with blue cheese.

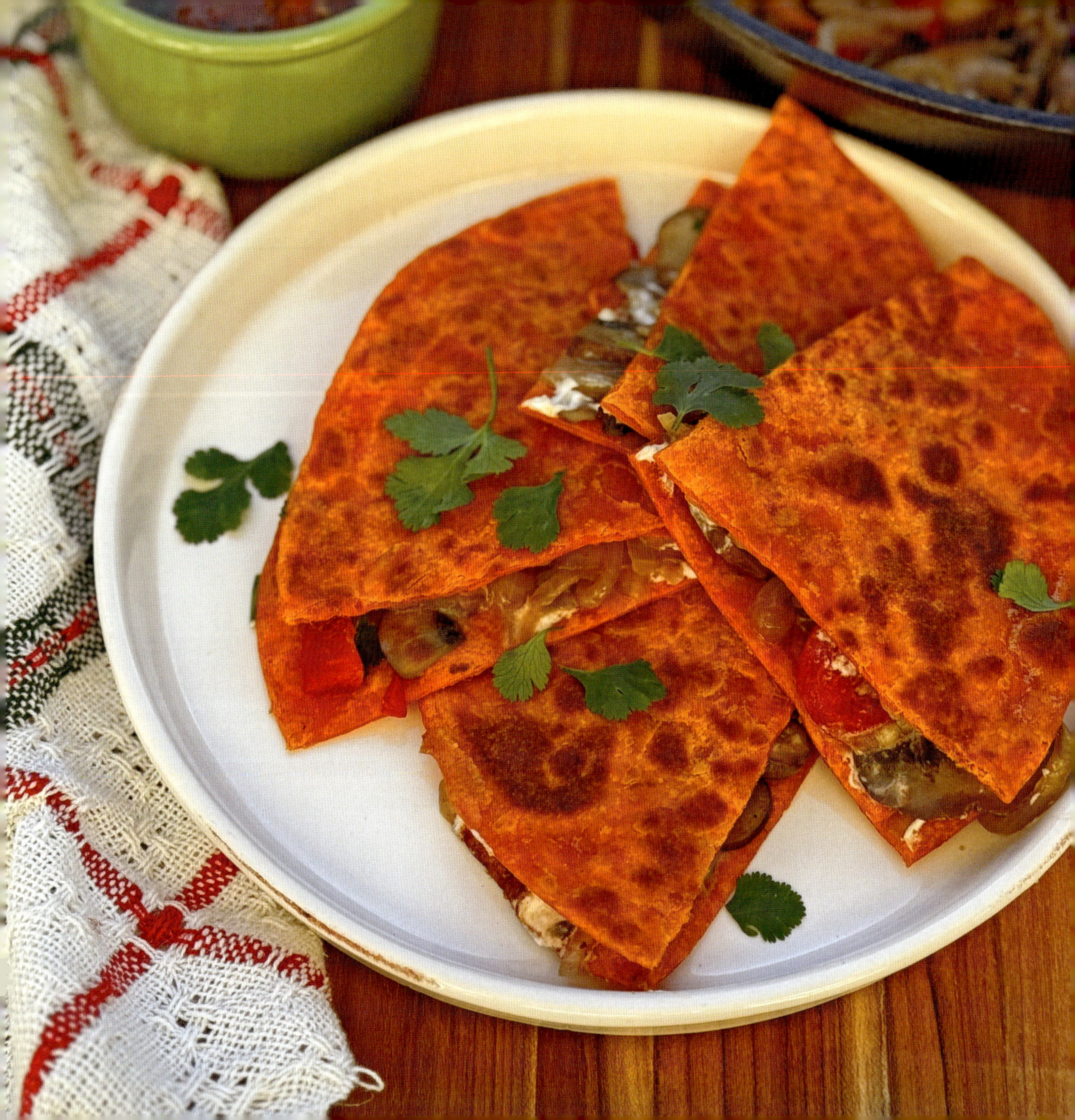

Mushroom-and-Onion Quesadillas

Try this delightful twist on a classic favorite, perfect for a quick weeknight dinner or a satisfying snack. Earthy mushrooms and sweet, smoky roasted red bell peppers pair beautifully with sautéed onions and gooey melted cheese, all tucked into crispy, golden tortillas. Serve with a dollop of sour cream, guacamole, or a zesty salsa for a simple-yet-flavorful dish that everyone will love.

makes 4 servings

INGREDIENTS

3 to 4 tablespoons butter, divided
8 ounces button or cremini mushrooms, sliced
½ onion, very thinly sliced
1 garlic clove, minced
1 roasted red bell pepper, thinly sliced
½ teaspoon ground cumin
¼ teaspoon ground coriander
½ teaspoon fine sea salt
½ teaspoon coarsely ground black pepper
¼ cup chopped fresh cilantro
8 (8-inch) flour tortillas, any flavor
1 cup (4 ounces) shredded Monterey Jack or cheddar cheese, divided
⅓ cup crumbled feta or goat cheese (optional)

TOPPINGS

fresh cilantro leaves, prepared salsa, guacamole, sour cream

Melt 2 tablespoons butter in a large skillet over medium heat. Add mushrooms and onion. Cook, stirring frequently, for 5 to 7 minutes or until tender. Stir in garlic, and cook for 1 minute.

Stir in red bell pepper, cumin, coriander, salt, and pepper. Stir in cilantro.

Place 4 tortillas on a flat surface. Sprinkle each evenly with ½ cup shredded cheese. Top evenly with mushroom mixture. Sprinkle with remaining ½ cup cheese and, if desired, feta. Top with remaining 4 tortillas.

Heat a griddle or large skillet over medium heat. Add remaining 1 tablespoon butter and let melt. Cook quesadillas for 1 to 2 minutes on each side, turning carefully. Cut into wedges and serve with desired toppings.

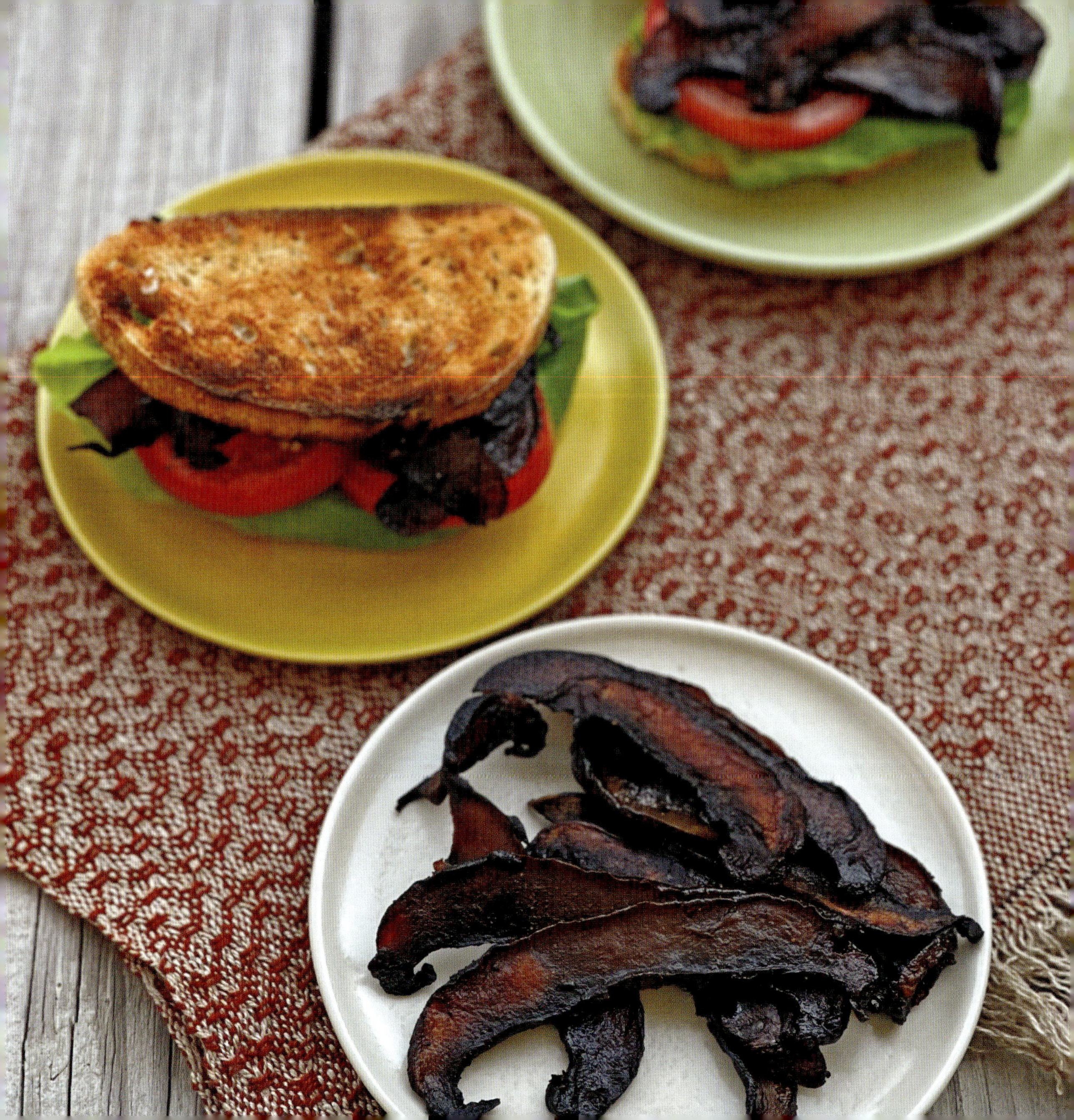

Portobello "Bacon," Lettuce, and Tomato Sandwiches

makes 6 servings

INGREDIENTS

1¼ to 1½ pounds portobello mushroom caps (about 4 extra-large)

⅓ cup extra-virgin olive oil

3 tablespoons maple syrup

3 tablespoons tamari or soy sauce

2 teaspoons hot sauce

1½ teaspoons liquid smoke

½ teaspoon fine sea salt

½ teaspoon garlic powder

12 slices sourdough bread, toasted

Mayonnaise

6 leaves Bibb, Romaine, or other lettuce

2 large tomatoes, sliced

Preheat oven to 375°. Line two rimmed baking sheets with parchment or nonstick aluminum foil.

Wipe mushrooms; clean and remove stems. Scoop away dark-brown gills underneath cap with a spoon and discard. Slice mushrooms about ⅛- to ¼-inch thick.

Spread mushrooms in a single layer in prepared pans. Combine oil, syrup, tamari, hot sauce, liquid smoke, salt, and garlic powder in a bowl. Brush marinade mixture on both sides of mushrooms. Drizzle any remaining liquid over top.

Bake for 30 minutes, rotating pans halfway through cooking time, or until mushrooms are tender and liquid evaporates.

Spread one side of bread slices with mayonnaise. Top 6 slices evenly with lettuce, tomato, mushroom bacon, and remaining 6 bread slices.

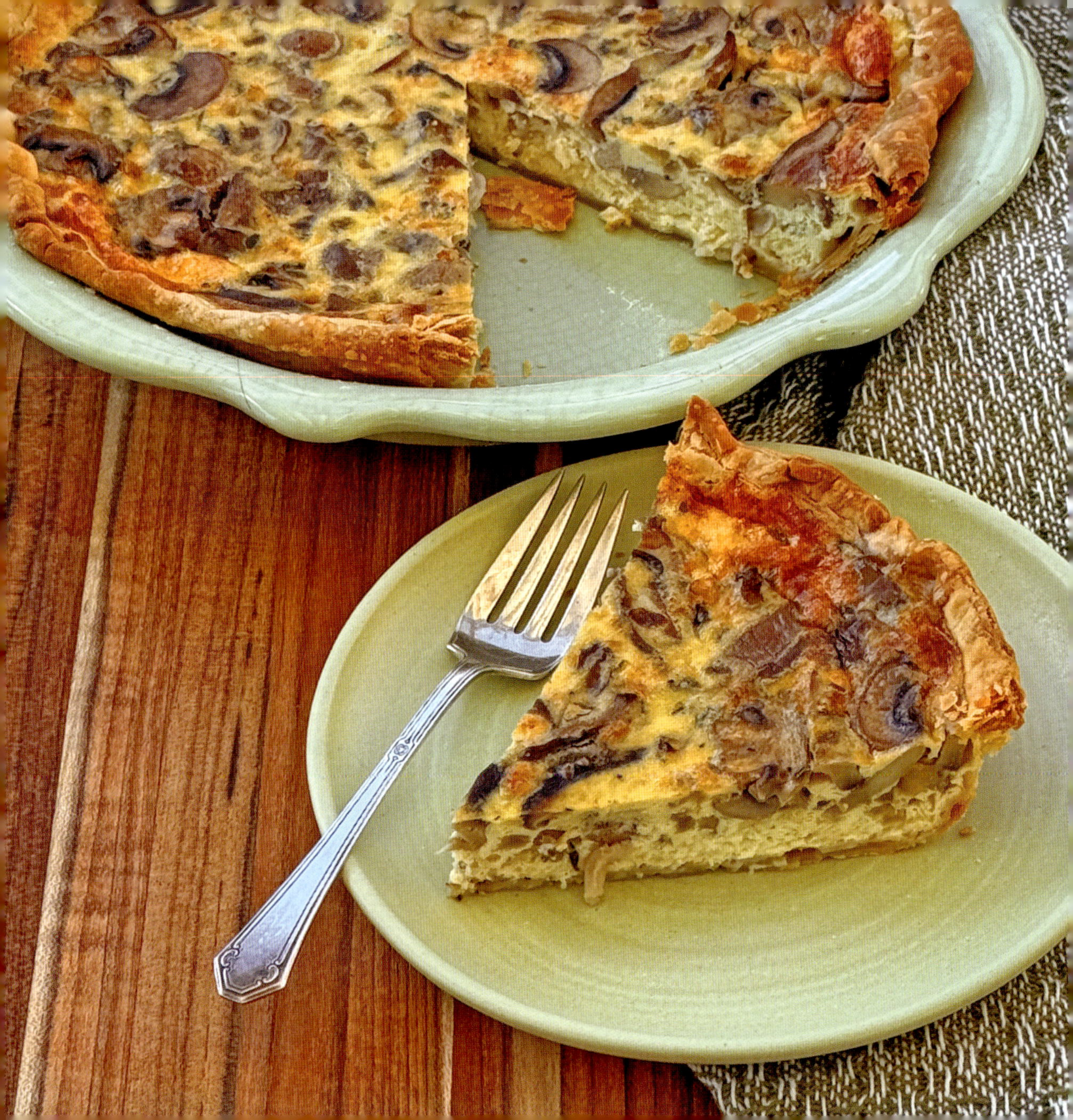

Mushroom Quiche

Perfect for brunch, lunch, or a light dinner, this quiche is versatile and impressive enough for special occasions yet simple enough for everyday enjoyment. Customize it with your favorite mushroom varieties and serve it alongside a crisp green salad or a bowl of seasonal soup for a satisfying meal.

makes 6 servings

INGREDIENTS

- 1 Pastry Crust (recipe at right) or 1 refrigerated piecrust
- ½ cup (2 ounces) shredded Swiss, cheddar, or Fontina cheese
- ¼ cup (1 ounce) freshly grated Parmesan cheese
- 2 tablespoons salted or unsalted butter
- 2 shallots, finely chopped
- 1 pound maitake, shiitake, oyster, cremini, or other mushroom, sliced
- 1 teaspoon chopped fresh thyme
- 4 large eggs
- ¾ teaspoon fine sea salt
- ½ teaspoon coarsely ground black pepper
- 1 cup half-and-half

Prepare pastry. Fit into a 9-inch shallow pie plate, crimping edges. Sprinkle Swiss and Parmesan cheese evenly into bottom of pie plate.

Preheat oven to 375°.

Melt butter in a large skillet over medium-high heat. Add shallots and mushrooms. Cook, stirring occasionally, for 8 to 10 minutes or until tender. Stir in thyme.

Whisk together eggs, salt, and pepper in a bowl. Whisk in half-and-half. Stir in mushroom mixture. Pour into piecrust.

Bake for 45 to 50 minutes or until golden brown and set.

Pastry Crust: Combine **1½ cups all-purpose flour** and **½ teaspoon salt** in a food processor; pulse until combined. Add **½ cup chilled butter,** cut into pieces; pulse until mixture resembles coarse meal. Drizzle **4 tablespoons water** over mixture; pulse until dough clumps together. Shape dough into a flat disk. Wrap in plastic and chill for 1 hour. Makes 1 piecrust.

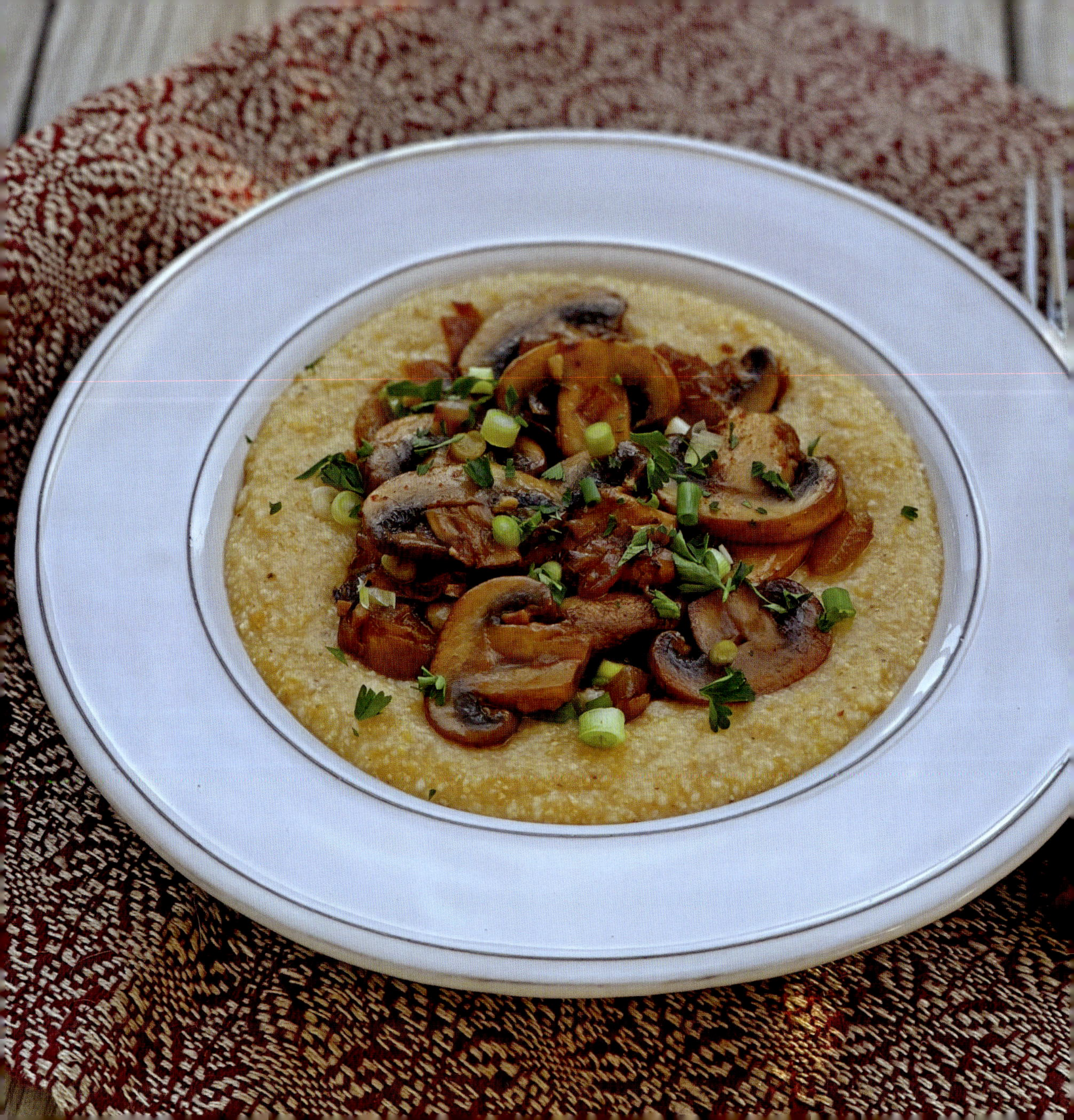

Sautéed Mushrooms with Grits

This recipe is a delightful take on the Southern classic, shrimp and grits. Richly sautéed mushrooms, cooked to a golden perfection with garlic and a splash of white wine, take center stage. Served over creamy, buttery grits, mushrooms provide a satisfying, vegetarian-friendly alternative to the traditional shrimp. Perfect for brunch, dinner, or anytime comfort food is calling, this dish is a celebration of Southern flavors with a modern, plant-based twist.

makes 4 servings

INGREDIENTS

2 tablespoons extra-virgin olive oil
2 tablespoons salted or unsalted butter
1 large onion, finely chopped
3 garlic cloves, minced
12 ounces assorted mushrooms (such as cremini, shiitake, and oyster), sliced
¼ cup dry white wine or vegetable broth
¼ teaspoon smoked paprika
¼ teaspoon cayenne pepper
½ teaspoon fine sea salt
½ teaspoon coarsely ground black pepper
Creamy Grits (recipe at right)

GARNISHES

chopped green onions, chopped fresh parsley

Heat olive oil and butter in a large skillet over medium heat. Add onion and cook, stirring frequently, for 3 to 4 minutes or until tender and translucent. Stir in garlic and cook for 1 minute or until fragrant.

Add mushrooms to skillet. Cook, stirring occasionally, for 8 to 10 minutes or until mushrooms release moisture and start to brown.

Add wine. Cook, scraping up browned bits from bottom of pan, for 2 to 3 minutes or until liquid is reduced by half. Stir in paprika, cayenne pepper, salt, and black pepper. Cook, stirring frequently, for 3 minutes.

Spoon Creamy Grits into bowls. Top with mushroom mixture and garnish, if desired.

Creamy Grits: Bring **4 cups vegetable broth, milk, or water** to a boil in a medium saucepan. Add **1 teaspoon salt** and **1 cup stone-ground grits**, whisking until smooth. Reduce heat and simmer, partially covered and stirring frequently, for 20 minutes or until grits are tender. Stir in **2 tablespoons butter, ½ cup grated cheddar cheese**, and **¼ cup heavy whipping cream**. Remove from heat and keep warm. Makes 5 cups.

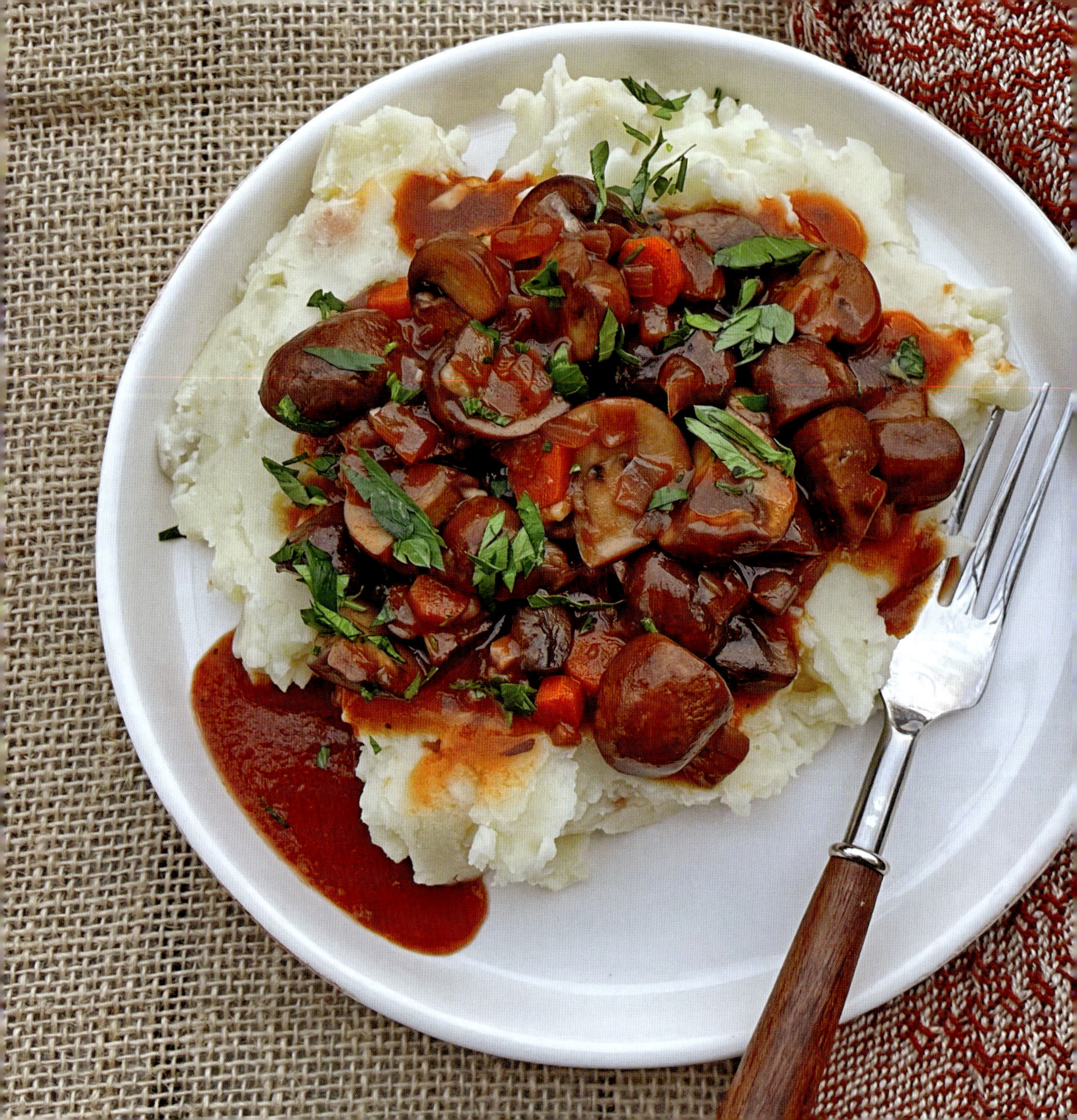

Mushroom Bourguignon

Using mushrooms instead of beef in this satisfying dish creates a rich, savory meal with a similar depth of flavor, thanks to the mushrooms' meaty texture. The mushrooms absorb the red wine and vegetable broth beautifully, resulting in a hearty vegetarian alternative.

makes 4 servings

INGREDIENTS

2 tablespoons extra-virgin olive oil, divided
1 tablespoon butter
1½ pounds mushrooms (cremini, button, or a mix), quartered
1 teaspoon fine sea salt, divided
½ teaspoon coarsely ground black pepper, divided
1 medium-size onion, diced
2 carrots, sliced
3 cloves garlic, minced
1 cup dry red wine (such as Burgundy)
2 cups vegetable broth
2 tablespoons tomato paste
1 tablespoon tamari or soy sauce
1 bay leaf
1 tablespoon all-purpose flour
2 tablespoons water
Hot mashed potatoes
2 tablespoons chopped fresh parsley

Heat 1 tablespoon olive oil and butter in a large skillet or Dutch oven over medium-high heat. Add mushrooms, ½ teaspoon salt, and ¼ teaspoon pepper. Cook for 7 to 10 minutes, stirring frequently, or until mushrooms are browned and liquid evaporates. Transfer mushrooms to a large plate and set aside.

Add remaining 1 tablespoon olive oil to skillet (no need to wipe clean). Add onion and carrots. Cook, stirring frequently, for 5 to 7 minutes or until tender. Stir in garlic and cook for 1 minute.

Pour wine into skillet, stirring to scrape up any browned bits from bottom of pan. Simmer for 5 minutes or until slightly reduced. Stir in broth, tomato paste, tamari, and bay leaf. Bring wine mixture to a simmer. Add reserved mushrooms back to pan. Simmer, uncovered, for 15 minutes.

Whisk flour with 2 tablespoons water in a small bowl. Stir flour mixture into mushroom mixture. Simmer for 2 minutes or until thickened. Stir in remaining ½ teaspoon salt and remaining ¼ teaspoon pepper. Remove and discard bay leaf before serving.

Serve over mashed potatoes and sprinkle with parsley.

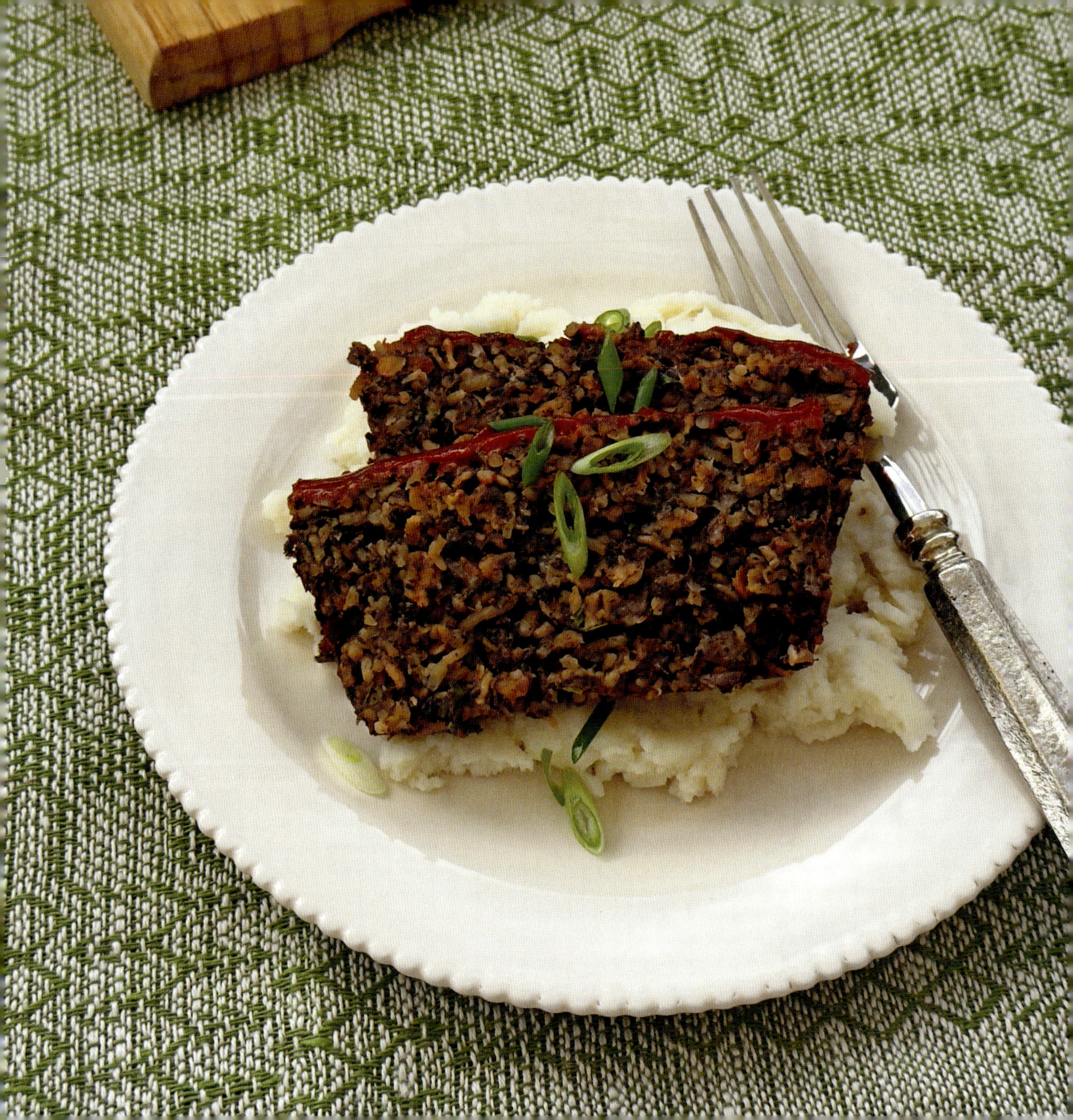

Vegetarian, Gluten-Free Portobello-Walnut "Meat" Loaf

If strict, make sure the Worcestershire is vegetarian (the original is not) and the tamari is gluten-free.

makes 4 servings

INGREDIENTS

2 tablespoons extra-virgin
   olive oil
1 pound (about 4 large)
   portobello mushroom caps
1 medium-size onion, chopped
2 garlic cloves, minced
1 teaspoon dried
   Italian seasoning
2 large eggs
1 cup chopped, toasted walnuts
1 cup cooked rice
½ cup gluten-free
   old-fashioned oats
½ cup (2 ounces) freshly grated
   or shredded Parmesan cheese
¼ cup chopped fresh parsley
1 tablespoon gluten-free tamari
1 tablespoon
   Worcestershire sauce
1¼ teaspoons fine sea salt
½ teaspoon coarsely ground
   black pepper
½ teaspoon smoked paprika
Glaze (recipe at right)
2 chopped green onions
Mashed potatoes

Preheat oven to 375°. Line an 8x4- or 9x4-inch loaf pan with parchment paper or nonstick aluminum foil.

Heat oil in a large skillet over medium heat. Chop mushrooms and add to skillet with onion, garlic, and Italian seasoning. Cook, stirring occasionally, for 7 to 9 minutes or until mushrooms are tender and have released almost all of their moisture.

Whisk eggs in a large bowl. Stir in walnuts, rice, oats, cheese, parsley, tamari, Worcestershire, salt, pepper, and paprika. Stir in mushroom mixture. Transfer to prepared loaf pan, smoothing top and pressing down lightly.

Bake for 20 minutes. Spread Glaze evenly over top and bake for 15 minutes or until loaf is heated through and set. Sprinkle with chopped green onions and serve with mashed potatoes.

Glaze: Combine **⅓ cup ketchup, 2 tablespoons dark or light brown sugar**, and **2 teaspoons Dijon mustard** in a small bowl. Makes ½ cup.

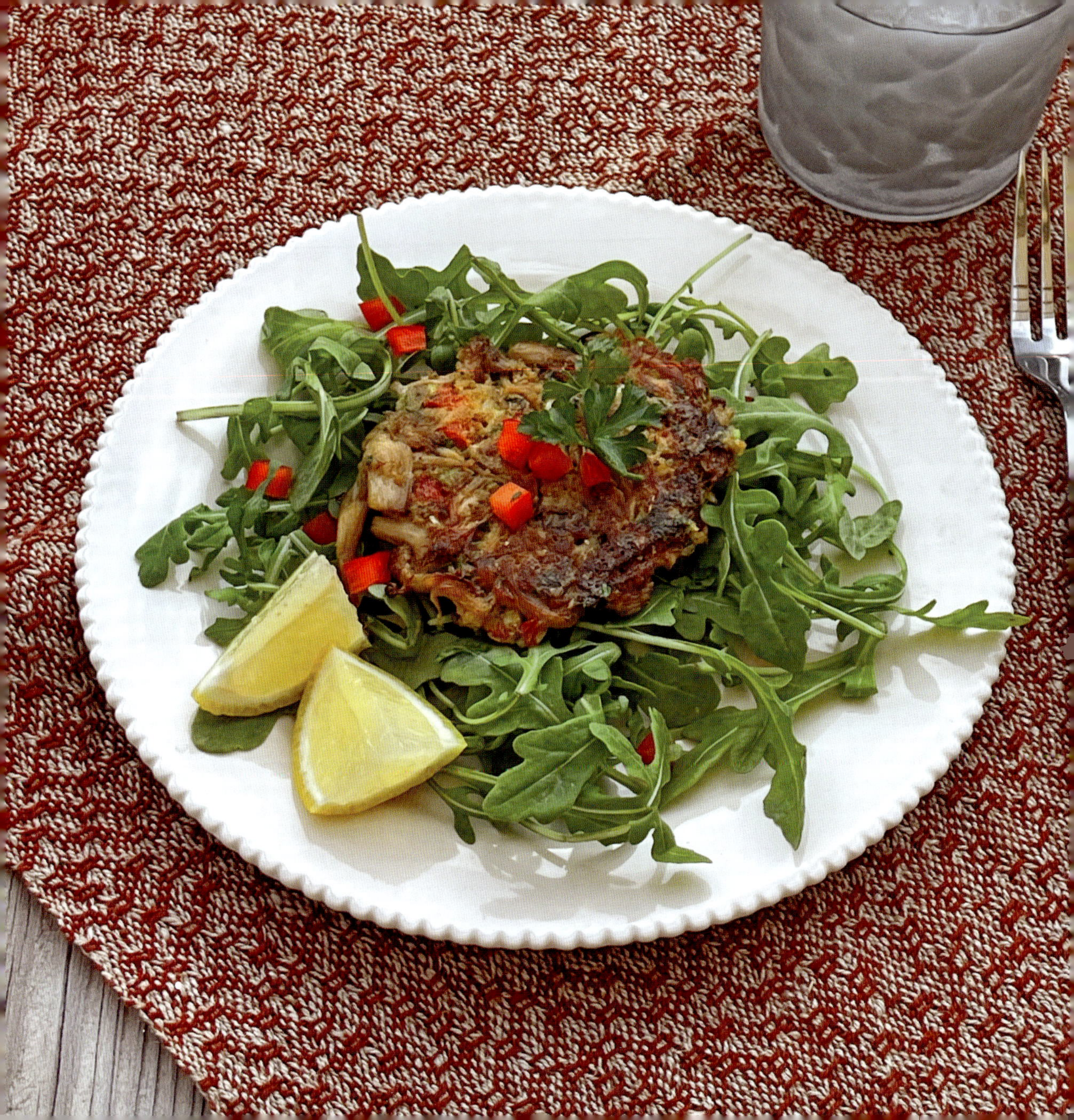

Lion's Mane Mushroom "Crab" Cakes

With their mildly sweet flavor, tender texture, and pale color, lion's mane mushrooms make an excellent substitute for crab and seafood in many recipes. Quickly cooking before assembling the cakes reduces the amount of water the mushrooms hold and improves digestibility. Season lightly so as not to overwhelm their delicate flavor.

makes 4 servings

INGREDIENTS

8 ounces lion's mane mushrooms
¼ cup minced red bell pepper
3 to 4 tablespoons water
1 large egg
2 green onions, minced
2 tablespoons chopped fresh
  parsley, cilantro, or dill
2 tablespoons mayonnaise
1 teaspoon Worcestershire sauce
½ teaspoon Dijon mustard
½ teaspoon seafood seasoning
¼ cup seasoned or plain fine
  breadcrumbs
Avocado or olive oil
Salad greens
Lemon wedges

Shred mushrooms into fine pieces similar to crabmeat. Combine shredded mushrooms, bell pepper, and 3 to 4 tablespoons water in a saucepan over medium heat. Bring to a boil. Reduce heat, and simmer, covered, for 4 to 5 minutes or until mushrooms and pepper are tender. Set aside to cool.

Drain mushroom mixture. Squeeze to remove excess water.

Whisk egg in a large bowl. Stir in green onions, parsley, mayonnaise, Worcestershire, Dijon, and seafood seasoning. Stir in breadcrumbs. Gently fold into mushroom mixture. Shape mixture into 4 cakes.

Pour a thin layer of oil in a large skillet over medium-high heat. Add cakes and cook for 2 to 3 minutes on each side or until golden brown. Serve over salad greens with lemon wedges.

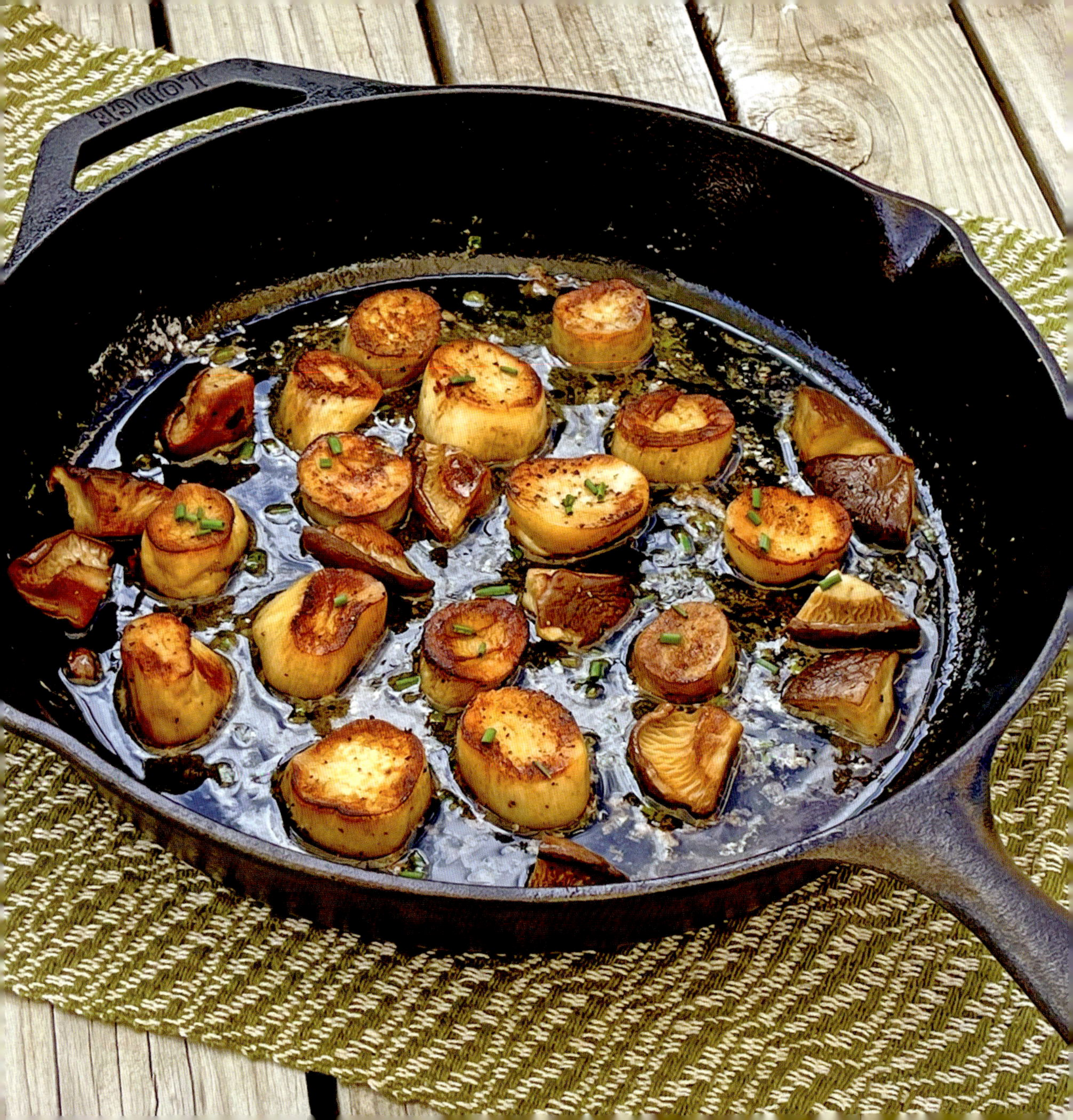

King Oyster "Scallops"

When sliced into thick rounds, the stems of these mushrooms closely resemble the look and texture of sea scallops. With a hot sear, they take on a golden crust and tender bite that mimics seafood beautifully. The subtle taste of king oyster mushrooms also allows them to absorb marinades and sauces well, making them perfect for a variety of dishes where scallops shine. Use the freshest oyster mushrooms you can find soon after purchasing because they tend to taste bitter with age. Pair this recipe with plain pasta or rice to soak up the delicious buttery sauce.

makes 4 servings

INGREDIENTS

6 large king oyster mushrooms (about 1 pound)
7 tablespoons melted salted or unsalted butter, divided
2 tablespoons plus 2 teaspoons lemon juice, divided
2 tablespoons soy or tamari sauce
¼ teaspoon smoked paprika
¼ teaspoon coarsely ground black pepper
2 tablespoons extra-virgin olive oil
¼ cup white wine
1 teaspoon chopped fresh chives

Trim ends of mushrooms and discard. Remove caps and quarter. Slice stems about ½-inch thick.

Combine 4 tablespoons melted butter, 2 tablespoons lemon juice, soy sauce, paprika, and pepper in a shallow bowl. Add mushrooms, tossing to coat. Let marinate for 30 minutes.

Heat a large cast-iron skillet over medium-high heat. Add oil and let heat. Add mushrooms, cut sides down, and cook for 2 to 3 minutes on each side. Transfer to a plate.

Add wine to skillet and cook for 1 minute or until liquid is almost evaporated. Remove from heat. Add remaining 3 tablespoons butter, remaining 2 teaspoons lemon juice, and chives. Return "scallops" to skillet and stir until coated in sauce.

Note: Some stores sell king oyster mushrooms already sliced lengthwise into planks. You can use them this way or cut in half to create squares.

Index

About the Author

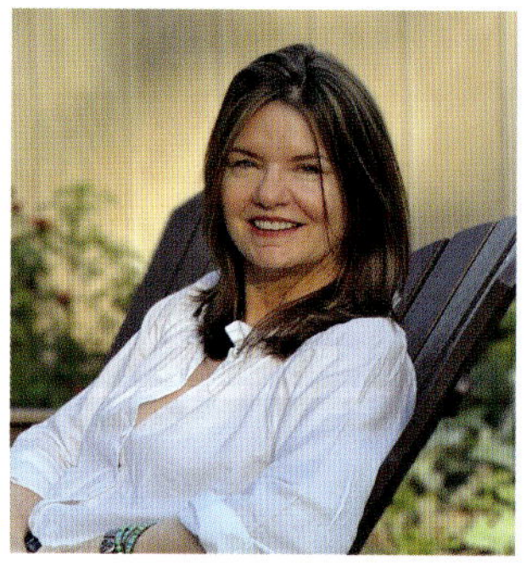

Julia Rutland is a writer and author with 25 years of experience in the food, publishing, travel, and marketing industries. She is the author of more than a dozen cookbooks, including *The Campfire Foodie Cookbook, On a Stick, Blueberries, Squash, Apples, Honey, Tomatoes, Eggs, Foil Pack Dinners, 101 Lasagnas, The Christmas Movie Cookbook, Homestyle Kitchen*, and *Cast-Iron Cooking*. Before moving to the Washington, D.C., area and developing her own business, Julia worked at *Coastal Living* magazine as senior food editor, with Wimmer Cookbooks as a sales and marketing consultant, and in the test kitchens of *Southern Living* magazine. Julia has a deep knowledge of cooking principles; she is passionate about consumer education and skilled in savvy story packaging. She is a member of Les Dames d'Escoffier, an international philanthropic organization of women leaders in the fields of food, fine beverage, and hospitality. Julia is also a trained volunteer and serves on the board with the Virginia Cooperative Extension Master Gardeners program in Loudon County. Julia lives in the D.C. wine-country town of Hillsboro, Virginia, with her husband, two daughters, and many furred and feathered friends.